Routledge Revivals

A Future for Africa

First published in 1992, *A Future for Africa* looks at the crises plaguing the Africa's societies and their economies and argues convincingly that the problems are not insuperable, but that, though their causes are largely external, the only long-term solutions rest in African hands.

In this book, the author shows how the adjustment programmes imposed on many African countries by the World Bank and the IMF have compounded the disastrous impact of foreign debt, trade restrictions and falling export prices. Real development will only be achieved, he maintains, by returning control of Africa's abundant resources to its people and by ensuring greater democracy and accountability in African political structures.

A Future for Africa

Beyond the Politics of Adjustment

Bade Onimode

Routledge Revivals
Routledge
Taylor & Francis Group

First published in 1992
by Earthscan Publications Ltd

This edition first published in 2025 by Routledge
4 Park Square, Milton Park, Abingdon, Oxon, OX14 4RN

and by Routledge
605 Third Avenue, New York, NY 10017

Routledge is an imprint of the Taylor & Francis Group, an informa business

Publisher's Note
The publisher has gone to great lengths to ensure the quality of this reprint but points out that some imperfections in the original copies may be apparent.

Disclaimer
The publisher has made every effort to trace copyright holders and welcomes correspondence from those they have been unable to contact.

A Library of Congress record exists under LCCN: 93104973

ISBN: 978-1-032-97864-2 (hbk)
ISBN: 978-1-003-59584-7 (ebk)
ISBN: 978-1-032-97865-9 (pbk)

Book DOI 10.4324/9781003595847

A future for Africa

Beyond the politics of adjustment

Bade Onimode

EARTHSCAN
Earthscan Publications Ltd, London
in association with the Institute for African Alternatives

First published 1992 by
Earthscan Publications Ltd
3 Endsleigh Street, London WC1H 0DD

British Library Cataloguing in Publication Data
Onimode, Bade
A Future for Africa: Beyond the politics of adjustment
1. Central Africa. Economic conditions
I. Title
330.467

ISBN 1-85383-100-X

Typeset by The Castlefield Press Limited, Wellingborough, Northants
Printed and bound by Biddles Ltd, Guildford and Kings Lynn

Earthscan Publications Ltd is an editorially independent subsidiary of Kogan Page Ltd, publishing in association with the International Institute for Environment and Development and the World Wide Fund for Nature (UK).

Contents

List of tables

Preface

This book makes the case for urgently relaunching Africa's development in the 1990s. It cautions against the increasing tendency to over-stretch the international debate on adjustment while neglecting the human and economic catastrophe on the continent. It directs policy action to the imperative of building an irreversible and sustained process of transformation on the painful ruins of the lost decade of the 1980s. Unless this is done immediately, with concerted political will and through sustained pressure from the people, Africa stands the real danger of also losing the 1990s and being counted out of the twenty-first century altogether.

The arguments are based on a view of adjustment politics as mere propaganda and point-scoring by the IMF, World Bank and their major sponsors in order to gain time and keep Africa down for as long as possible. This would provide them with an opportunity to exploit Africa's enormous resources for dealing with the Asian Challenge to Western hegemony, and to deny Africa any effective role in world economy and global affairs. It is the implementation of a *political strategy* for the recolonisation of Africa and the rest of the Third World within the current offensive of world capitalism and the global restructuring of capital through the creation of regional economic blocs in North America, Europe and Pacific Asia. The thinly disguised politicking with external debt crisis and Structural Adjustment Programmes (SAPs) makes this abundantly clear.

Thus the external debt crisis has been called a '*Financial Low Intensity Conflict*' (FLIC), while the ganging up of the so-called creditor countries in the Club of London and Club of Paris negates the market theology being preached by these Club members. It is against this background that this book maintains that the external debt has been repaid in net capital outflow of over $200 billion from Africa and the rest of the Third World to the North in the 1980s alone: the colossal loss of export earnings from the collapse of commodity trade; additional losses from falling terms of trade; huge profit repatriation by transnational corporations; losses of external reserves due to foreign exchange fluctuations and related sources. Hence Africa must demand reparations payment for the loss of some 70 million lives during slavery, colonialism and neocolonialism in order to underscore the fact that Africa is a net creditor to the world economy and not a debtor.

Similarly, the rapid spread of conditionality to all aspects of economic relations between Africa and the West – from the IMF to the World Bank, the Lomé Convention between EEC and ACP countries, and even to drawing from the newly created International Commodity Fund – testifies to the true character of adjustment politics. It is reflected in the dogmatic and rigid insistence of the Bretton Woods institutions on extortionate debt collection; harsh cross-conditionalities and the oppressive implementation of SAPs. This continues in spite of abundant evidence that these programmes have failed tragically, are systematically destroying African economies and societies, and in spite of the Bank's own admission that the SAPs are experimental.

This book maintains, however, that the adjustment debate has been useful in some ways. It has compelled the collection of empirical evidence on the practical impact of IMF and World Bank orthodox SAPs on economic, social and political conditions in African countries. The highlighting of the fallacies of specific adjustment policies is another benefit. More important, the adjustment debate has encouraged the formulation of alternative recovery programmes as shown by the ECA's *African Alternative*.

In order to transcend the politics of adjustment in Africa, this book calls for the urgent termination of the World Bank's parallelism in publishing alternatives to African blueprints, rather than assisting and supporting African countries to implement their own programmes – as the Bank claims repeatedly that it wants to do. On their part, African countries and their leaders must stop the habit of proclaiming one thing and practising another – they must develop the self-confidence, courage and dignity to implement their own programmes and blueprints, no matter what outsiders may do or say. Thus if the Lagos Plan of Action (LPA) had been implemented even partially, the current crisis would have been less severe, if not averted altogether. The abiding lesson is that only Africans themselves can develop Africa – outsiders can only assist and support, and so they must never be allowed to supplant and displace Africa's own initiatives.

Hence the second coming of Africa – its second liberation – must be anchored firmly to the urgent implementation of the revised Lagos Plan of Action and its Treaty of the African Economic Community; the African Alternative (AAF-SAP); and the African Charter for Popular Participation in Development. Africa must seize its new historic moment to launch an irreversible and sustainable programme of structural transformation from a political foundation of democratic popular participation and effective accountability at all levels.

Bade Onimode
Ibadan
April 30, 1991.

Chapter 1
Introduction

The debate over orthodox stabilization and adjustment to the African crisis has been on for a decade. In the course of it, the crisis and the IMF and World Bank Stabilization and Structural Adjustment Programmes (SAPs) have generated and exacerbated a serious decline in the African economy, and created the catastrophe of suffering facing the rural and urban poor, women, children, workers, peasants and other vulnerable social groups. A generation of Africans has been lost and a second is under serious threat, while the marginalization of Africa has accelerated alarmingly in most spheres.

It is time, therefore, to transcend the politics of adjustment and move urgently forward to implement the agreed policies and priorities that have emerged from the controversy. This is imperative in order to prevent the politics of adjustment from compromising the necessary adjustment-with-transformation of African countries. After the lost decade of the 1980s, Africa's development process must be relaunched and resumed. The beginning of the 1990s must curb its steep decline, and halt the involuntary de-linking of the coach of the African region from the speeding locomotive of the global economy. Full agreement is not necessary, and may not be possible, on all issues of the protracted controversy surrounding Africa's external debt, crisis and adjustment. But enough has been said to point the way ahead and move the African agenda forward on the points of agreement that have been reached.

Beyond the new colonialism

The 1990s are widely regarded as the final era of the new colonialism, in much the same way as the 1960s marked the beginning of the modern era in the region's history. The salient point of the analogy is that this decade must mark the termination of the new economic bondage of the region under the IMF and World Bank's orthodox SAPs. Indeed, the external debt crisis and its doctrinaire SAPs represent the "new colonialism" in Africa under the close supervision of the IMF and World Bank, and can be seen as the stage of financial imperialism in the broad sweep of imperial history. It follows the multilateral stage of imperialism under the reign of multinational corporations from the end of the Second World War to the end of the 1970s.

The new era in Africa from the 1990s must thus represent the end of this recolonization, which has taken place under the rubric of the politics of adjustment. Transcending the adjustment debate at the conceptual level, alternative policies and programmes must replace these new colonial relationships of exploitation and domination represented by Africa's external debt, and the IMF and World Bank SAPs. Unless there is a resolution of the foreign debt crisis that releases additional resources to African countries and a concomitant phasing-out of orthodox SAPs, it will neither be possible to find adequate resources to relaunch Africa's development process, nor to put alternative recovery and development programmes into place. Underlying this, the politics of adjustment reveal that both the SAPs and the external debt crisis are integral components of a *political strategy* designed to recolonize Africa, keep it down and deny it effective participation in world affairs. This thesis is elaborated in Chapter 3.

Hence the beginning of the 1990s must see a decisive relaxation of the external debt constraint on Africa's development and the replacement of current orthodox SAPs with more appropriate programmes of adjustment-with-transformation. This requires a clear political focus on the adjustment controversies of the 1980s. The priority issues are as follows:

- Nature of the African crisis;
- The external debt problem;
- Relevance and impact of IMF-World Bank imposed SAPs;
- Africa's collapsed commodity trade;
- Democratization and the Western agenda;
- The World Bank's long-term perspective study (LTPS, 1989) and "new generation" SAPs;
- Possible impact of the Uruguay Round of GATT negotiations on Africa.

The controversies over these issues cut across national boundaries, regional interests and international institutions. Within each country, sub-region and Africa as a whole, there are supporters and critics of adjustment, just as there are within the international community, the IMF and the World Bank. These individuals, groups and institutions on all sides of the adjustment debate are found in both the South and the North. Broadly speaking, however, the beneficiaries of the adjustment process in each country, within the Africa region and in the international community have tended also to be the advocates of different aspects of adjustment, while their opponents have tended to be the victims of the process and their supporters and sympathizers. Like any political arena, the politics of adjustment involves not only conflicting ideas, but also a struggle over resources.

Within the adjustment controversy, three broad positions can be identified. There are those who actively defend orthodox adjustment programmes without major changes; supporters and critics who advocate major modifications to the current programmes, for example, extension of programmes from the short-run to the medium-term; and those who consider orthodox SAPs as fundamentally flawed, having failed empirically and additionally, inappropriate for Africa. This text concerns the two poles of opinion with respect to the seven issues listed above.

These issues, and the surrounding controversies, have (or will, in the case of LTPS and Uruguay Round of GATT) contributed to the intensification of the regional crisis. But they also involve areas of consensus with respect to desired changes in policy. Until these are translated into practical policies and programmes on the ground, however, the rhetoric of consensus remains a benign echo of the politics of adjustment. Taking one example, the World Bank's LTPS identifies the need for adjustment-with-growth, human-centred development, human resource development, satisfaction of critical needs in food, education, health, etc., flexible uses of market forces and prices, pragmatic balancing of public and private sectors, regional food security, African integration and industrialization. But it has persistently failed to initiate corresponding programmes or projects, or to support the implementation of alternative programmes to satisfy these needs.

Instead the IMF and World Bank strategy has been that African countries must first achieve financial stabilization before resuming economic growth. This is the logic of the quick-fix one or two-year stabilization and adjustment programmes, which have failed disastrously. As this stabilization is sought in financial variables like budgets, credit, money supply, market prices, foreign exchange rates and reserves, it is clear that it will not eliminate the root causes of the African crisis. These are the inherited perverse colonial patterns of production, consumption, distribution, technology and power. The misguided and futile search for financial stabilization in the past has aggravated the crisis and undermined the recovery process through massive foreign debt payments, destruction of human resources, brain drain, excessive inflation from massive generalized devaluation and crippling of domestic production. Moreover, as this search for financial stabilization has proved elusive for over ten years, Africa can no longer keep its transformation on hold. Hence though financial stabilization is desirable, it must be pursued alongside accelerated development and transformation.

Some argue that adjustment should not be the fundamental objective of Africa's political economy at this historical juncture, but that each country should be left to pursue its own national programme of crisis management. They point to the fact that several African countries, such as Nigeria, Tanzania and Zambia, had indeed started implementing such national programmes with varying degrees of success. Where such programmes failed to contain the crisis, this was not so much because they were inherently faulty, but because they could not get external support for implementing them effectively.

Others argue that adjustment is an external requirement and not logically related to the internal dynamics of the crisis. They maintain that, as long as African countries remain within the orbit of the international capitalist system, they cannot escape periodic crises that spill over from the crises of the core capitalist countries. To deal with the situation, what is required is not externally imposed adjustment, but programmes to insulate African economies from the fluctuations of world capitalism. They require structural disengagement, or de-linking from the international capitalist system, in the pursuit of relative autonomy for the national economy to achieve its legitimate priorities. Supporters of the dependency school, and others arguing for national economic independence for Third World countries, press this argument. For them, adjustment is an ideological imposition and not just a matter of all countries adjusting to changing economic situations.

The global context

The current global context adds urgency to the imperative of transcending the politics of adjustment. This is the setting of the "megatrends to year 2000". The major developments to which Africa must rapidly respond include the dramatic reforms in Eastern Europe; East-West détente; the reorganization of NATO and the Warsaw pact with new security arrangements for Europe; the world democratic revolution; the emerging regional economic blocs in Europe, North America and the Pacific Rim; the current technological revolution in informatics, biotechnology and genetic engineering; the recent Gulf crisis and the new security arrangements for the Middle East; the liberation of Southern Africa; and the increasing marginalization of Africa in world affairs.

These major global transformations define the context to which Africa has been adjusting since the 1980s, and in which it must seek transformation throughout the 1990s. These changes pose serious problems for Africa, but they also offer important opportunities. On the negative side, the reforms in Eastern Europe jeopardize much of the technical assistance and international support which these countries used to offer so generously to African countries, especially those pursuing socialist policies. Europe 1992 will also mean the end of significant export preferences and concessions, especially for agricultural and other products. The establishment of the European Monetary System (EMS) is also likely to diminish French support for CFA zone countries within the franc currency union. Other regional economic blocs are likely to constitute additional foreign trade barriers for Africa, while recent technological advances allow increased synthetic substitution for Africa's raw materials. The Gulf crisis has also increased Africa's import burden by an estimated $20 billion, according to the preliminary figures of the UN General Assembly. But, on the positive side, these global transformations have given a new fillip to Africa's democratization, provided additional incentives for increasing the competitiveness of its exports and diversifying them, while increasing regionalism should intensify closer cooperation among African countries.

To respond effectively and in time, African economies and societies must undergo accelerated recovery-with-transformation. This is clearly impossible within the constraints of the present politics of adjustment, with its crippling external debt and failed orthodox SAPs. The fundamental strategy needed for Africa's response to these global changes is effective African integration of its fragmented markets and production systems. This is not possible with the atomistic country-by-country strategy of on-going SAPs, which undermine the harmonization of policies and programmes among countries, while the debt overhang continues to deny the resources needed for integrative regional programmes. Related issues like the collapse of Africa's commodity trade, the imperative of full democratization and the impact of the Uruguay Round of GATT also have to be tackled for Africa to adjust effectively to the emerging global realignment.

Chapter 2 analyses the internal and external causes of the African crisis as a background to the elaboration of feasible solutions. The politics of the African foreign debt crisis is examined in Chapter 3, which includes a discussion of Africa's demand for reparations payment for past depredations of the continent. The full debate over stabilization and adjustment is discussed in Chapter 4. This is followed by the presentation in Chapter 5 of the African alternative to orthodox SAPs and the strategy for its implementation. Chapter 6 discusses the central question of the necessity for democratic participation in the adjustment and transformation process in Africa. The various options for transcending the politics of adjustment are then analysed in Chapter 7. The final chapter concludes with an overview of Africa's second coming in a world in transition – the challenges and the opportunities.

Chapter 2

Internal and external causes of the crisis

The nature of the crisis

It is by now clear that the African crisis is not only economic, but also political and social. This is with respect to both causes and manifestations. Thus as one of the underlying problems of underdevelopment, the pervasive lack of democracy in the region has been described by some in terms of "how politics underdevelops Africa". The catastrophic social impact of the crisis has also been widely accepted, but important social factors like corruption or the perverse bias of official policy against the rural areas and populations, as well as class and ethnic conflicts, have augmented the severity of the crisis in several countries.

Similarly, it is difficult to explain the crisis using conventional theories, whether bourgeois or Marxian. Bourgeois theories of business cycles, like the deficient aggregate demand of Keynes, the monetary or credit theory of von Hayek or the inventory model of Hicks do not explain the critical aspects of crises in the Third World. The Marxian theories of under-consumption, over-production or falling rate of profit also fail to explain adequately the character of socio-economic crises in Africa and the rest of the Third World (Onimode, 1989). But these theories do offer useful analytical tools for developing alternative theories to explain these crises. The Marxian theory of disproportionality or unbalanced sectoral growth is particularly useful for its insights into the imbalances between agriculture and the rest of the economy, which contributed to the agrarian crisis in Africa; the imbalance between the dominant external sector and the rest of the economy in African countries where "the tail wags the dog"; and the disproportionality between the predominant oil sector and the rest of the economy in oil-exporting countries.

However, there remains the need to formulate holistic theories for explaining the socio-economic crises in Africa and the rest of the Third World. But first it is necessary to identify the causes of the current crisis to formulate appropriate restorative policies. This chapter contributes to this more modest task, discussing the internal and external causes of the crisis. These have generated an intense debate between the IMF and World Bank, among others, and some of their major sponsors, who insist against all evidence that the crisis has been caused primarily by internal factors, and others in Africa and elsewhere who find external factors the dominant culprits. The main internal and external causes will therefore be examined before their relative weights are evaluated.

Internal causes

Domestic policy failures in African countries have contributed to the African crisis, whether in the form of the agrarian crisis, the external debt problem or general socio-economic decline. These policy failures have occurred mainly in five broad areas, the first of which was the failure to change the inherited perverse colonial economic and socio-political structures, in particular the authoritarian colonial state. Economically, colonialism programmed African countries to consume what they do not produce and to produce what they do not consume. This was most noticeable in agriculture and mining. In the agricultural sector, colonial regimes imposed compulsory cropping and Africans were forced to concentrate on the production of "cash crops" – cotton, rubber, tea, coffee, cocoa – to meet the raw material requirements of the factories of Europe. Domestic food production was systematically neglected because the colonialists did not consume African foodstuffs. This pattern was retained by post-colonial regimes, especially as their demand for foreign exchange could only be met through the production and export of these "cash crops".

In the mining sector, the colonial regimes encouraged the domestic production of minerals for export to meet the reproductive requirements of their economies. This was how Central and Southern Africa became huge mining concessions, and mineral exploitation became a priority in other parts of Africa. But there was minimal domestic utilization or processing of these minerals in Africa.

Manufacturing activities did not develop in colonial Africa, for similar reasons. Indeed, the colonial regimes promptly eliminated pre-colonial manufacturing activities in textiles, soap, iron and leather by shipping their raw materials to Europe and replacing their products with manufactured goods, destroying the market for domestic manufacturing. In countries like Nigeria, Tanzania and Kenya, colonial regimes deliberately banned domestic manufacturing by prohibiting the local fabrication of raw materials. With their sources of supply and demand eliminated – and their skilled artisans drafted into forced labour or wage labour through the imposition of monetary taxes – the domestic manufacturing activities simply collapsed. This process of systematic de-industrialization of Africa is now being repeated under Structural Adjustment Programmes (SAPs) which impede access to foreign supplies of spare parts and raw materials for local industries, and displace the demand for local manufactures through the dumping of foreign manufactures in the name of import liberalization, a cause to be expanded by the Uruguay Round of GATT.

Similarly, the authoritarian colonial state and its denial of democracy has been retained in the form of the authoritarian post-colonial state in Africa. This law-and-order state is repressive and incapable of mobilizing a national population for development. Chronic internal conflicts have been provoked all over Africa by this undemocratic and alienating post-colonial state. Correspondingly, colonialism bequeathed a profound confusion of values and institutions to the whole of Africa through its systematic deformation of African society. It did not completely destroy the pre-colonial society, nor did it completely build modern capitalist societies. It was neither as fully destructive nor as fully regenerative as Marx had predicted in his study of colonialism in India (Marx, 1970), in which he thought that colonialism would destroy largely feudal (Asiatic) pre-colonial society and regenerate it as a modern capitalist society.

Post-colonial Africa has failed to transform these inherited structures of production, consumption, distribution, technology, power, institutions and values. It was wrongly assumed that these structures could be used as a basis for nation-building and the development of African economies and societies. The maturing contradictions of this error have contributed to the agrarian crisis, socio-economic stagnation and decline as well as political strife throughout Africa.

Partly for these reasons and because of the flaw in imported modernization theory, there has been a systematic anti-rural bias in official policy. The neglect of food production encouraged the benign neglect of rural areas and populations, which has contributed to the collapse of the rural economy, the generation of the agrarian crisis, rural-urban drift and unemployment. As imported modernization theory extolled the virtues and supremacy of the so-called modern sectors and values, this biased official policy towards the urban areas, the parasitic élites and such "modern" activities as commerce, banking and industry. The result has been a built-in commitment to disproportionality or the absence of balanced development. Other failures, like poor agricultural pricing, inability to mobilize domestic savings and other resources, or to mobilize national populations either to implement development programmes or even to defend African countries against external interventions, can all be traced to this bias against the rural majority – and in turn have all contributed to the current crisis.

African countries have unduly large unproductive investment activity expenditures, as shown in Table 2.1. These "white elephant" projects include stadia, conference centres, sports festivals and poorly costed and mismanaged projects across various sectors of the economy. The huge annual losses of unprofitable parastatals or public enterprises are a good example of this. Besides distorted national priorities, due partly to lack of democratic participation in the choice of these national priorities, there is also excessive politicization of essentially technical and economic questions. Thus the distortion of development plans with the arbitrary addition of uncosted projects, execution of these unviable projects following political interference in choice of location and routine management, and similar abuses contribute to this unproductive investment, the fiscal crisis of the state and the generation of the current crisis. Excessive defence expenditure of around 5 billion annually is an egregious example of this unproductive spending in African countries, and much African external debt has been due to the foreign procurement of armaments. As resources are increasingly diverted to defence, investment in education and health for human resource development, agriculture, industry, infrastructure etc. suffer (see Table 2.2). But the point should also be made that much of this excessive defence spending is often necessitated by foreign interventions in African countries.

Table 2.1: Unproductive investment in Africa – net rates of return on capital

Region	1961–73	1973–80	1980–87
Sub-Saharan Africa	83.8	23.5	6.2
South Asia	47.8	38.5	36.5

Source: World Bank, *Sub-Saharan Africa: From Crisis to Sustainable Growth – A Long-term Perspective Study,* LTPS, 1989, p. 26.

Gross economic mismanagement, corruption and capital flight have also contributed to the crisis (Naylor, 1988). These are facilitated by the undemocratic character of the post-colonial state, which typically comprises small cliques in power. With authoritarian powers and no accountability, these cliques can systematically loot their countries,

Table 2.2(a): Expenditure on defence, education and health as percentage of total government spending in selected countries, 1987

Country	Defence	Education	Health
Burkina Faso	17.3	19.0	5.8
Kenya	9.1	23.1	6.6
Liberia	8.9	16.2	7.1
Malawi	6.6	10.8	7.1
Morocco	14.5	16.9	2.9
Tanzania	15.8	8.3	5.7
Uganda	26.3	15.0	2.4
Zaire (1986)	5.2	0.8	1.8

Table 2.2(b): Defence spending as percentage of total government expenditure

	1980	1981	1985	1986
Sub-Saharan Africa	12.1	11.7	10.0	–
Ethiopia	30.0	34.0	34.6	32.0
Uganda	25.2	31.2	15.6	26.3
Zimbabwe	25.0	20.5	15.2	16.3
Somalia	19.2	22.7	–	–
Burkina Faso	17.0	18.4	19.2	18.3
Kenya	16.4	10.7	8.7	10.6
Senegal	16.8	11.8	10.8	10.6
Sudan	13.2	12.3	12.2	10.2

Sources: World Bank, *World Development Report,* 1987; World Bank, *LTPS,* p. 168.

diverting billions of dollars of state funds into private foreign bank accounts and property accumulation. This corruption encourages unproductive spending on large contracts (often with kick-back) and such inflated contracts make it impossible to ensure the efficient management of enterprises and resources. Excessive deficit financing due to excessive borrowing from internal and external sources, as well as poor financial control, are additional aspects of this mismanagement pervasive in most African countries.

Perverse politics has contributed to the escalation of the crisis in several ways. Stemming from the authoritarian and alienating character of a post-colonial state incapable of sustained resource mobilization and allocation for development, these include the resultant internal conflicts and instability; the pervasive lack of democracy and popular participation; the consequent lack of political and financial accountability and the resulting abuse of power, especially for corrupt private accumulation.

But the point must be made that these domestic policy failures have not always been caused solely by internal factors: external forces have played an important role. This is particularly the case with the retention of the colonial economic system, whose agricultural sector was rationalised by advice from the World Bank – for example, the World Bank mission to Nigeria under colonialism in 1953 sanctioned the system. Similarly, corruption and excessive defence spending have always been aided and abetted by foreign collaborators. Many Western countries systematically install and support dictatorial regimes that subvert democracy in many African countries. This is, however, not to deny the responsibility of Africans themselves, especially the leaders and elites, for these failures.

External causes

Indeed, several external causes greatly contributed to the emergence and intensification of the African crisis. The most important of these was the dramatic collapse of Africa's commodity exports, in both volume and prices, in the 1980s. This was due largely to virulent protectionism, especially in the USA; increasing synthetic substitution of raw materials through the development of biotechnology and genetic engineering; the collapse of international commodity agreements; and the economic crisis in the industrialized countries in the 1980s. Even as recently as 1989, the International Coffee Agreement collapsed and coffee prices fell by about 19 per cent to their lowest level in 14 years.

As a result of these adverse export developments, Africa lost $19 billion in export earnings in one year during 1985-86 alone. the terms of trade have also fallen sharply, as shown in Table 2.3.

Table 2.3: Africa's declining terms of trade (1980 = 100)

1970	1975	1985	1986	1987	1988
81	78	96	65	66	60

Source: African Development Bank (ADB), *African Development Report 1990* (Abidjan), p. 174.

When it is appreciated that most African countries have such excessive export concentration that one or two export commodities account for 70–90 per cent of total export earnings, which in turn account for over 80 per cent of total annual government revenue, the enormous and pernicious implications of this export collapse become truly alarming.

Just as export earnings were plummeting and balance of payments crises were escalating, foreign lending conditions were also deteriorating. Soft concessional lending at low interest rates began to dry up and countries were forced to borrow from private sources on increasingly disadvantageous terms. Thus the overall duration of foreign loans decreased from 10–20 years to about five years; the grace period before loan repayment became shorter; and the loan repayment period was sharply reduced. As a result, it became increasingly difficult to repay or service loans for long-gestation projects like agricultural exports such as cocoa, coffee, tea, rubber and palm produce, which required about eight years to produce and market.

Sharply rising interest rates then compounded these repayment problems. While the average interest rates on external loans used to be around three to five per cent in the sixties, they shot up to between 10 and 17 per cent in the 1970s. Worse still, these rates were made variable so that rising interest rates were even applied to past loans. Thus with Africa's total external debt of around $250 billion by the end of 1990, if the interest rate rises by one per cent, the *additional* debt burden on Africa would rise by $2.5 billion – without any additional loans or inflow of foreign capital. What is even more ominous is the higher likelihood that when rising interest rates are applied to past loans taken at a five per cent interest rate, they would suddenly have to be repaid with around 17 per cent interest. Massive deficit financing under the Reagan administration in the US contributed much to these rising interest rates, thus passing part of the cost of US spending on to the rest of the world, via infrastructural loans for building roads, dams, etc., and agricultural loans for export production. Such loans thus become virtually unrepayable due to insufficient economic returns, especially since the 1980s' collapse of export prices and volumes.

The practices of the international banks have also contributed directly to the external debt crisis, and hence to the overall crisis. As external creditors, these banks exercise great power over debtor countries. Besides sharply raising interest rates, they have typically depressed the credit worthiness of African and other Third World countries, diminished their access to foreign credit, and raised financial charges against them. These practices, combined with the rapid deterioration of export earnings have severely aggravated the crisis in African countries.

Equally serious is the impact of the multinational corporations (MNCs') activities in generating and intensifying the regional crisis through massive de-capitalization, technological retardation and local displacement. Increasing evidence points to significant MNC contributions to the net export of capital from Third World countries. The total value of this net outflow of resources from the South to the North was estimated at around $156 billion between 1985 and 1990, or about $31 billion annually. The net outflow of resources from Africa is shown in Table 2.5. These net resource outflows include over $1 billion annually to the World Bank and IMF – in spite of their virtuous rhetoric about helping Africa out of the crisis. The MNCs' contribution to this net resource outflow from Africa is made through the repatriation of super-profits that appear as "investment income" in the balance of payments and through transfer pricing or the over-invoicing of imports and the under-invoicing of exports. Thus from Nigeria alone, the net capital transfer by the MNCs was about $3.9 billion between 1970 and 1980[1]. The UN Commission on Transnational Corporations (UNCTC) has studied the resource transfer through transfer pricing by the MNCs.

MNCs contribution to technological retardation by monopolizing global technology, restricting access to it by Africa and the rest of the Third World under the system of industrial property rights of patents, trade-marks, copyrights, etc., charging exploitative monopoly prices or rent for it and transferring inappropriate and relatively capital-intensive technologies rather than relatively labour-intensive technologies to these labour-abundant countries (Vaitsos, 1970). The result has been the persistent failure of the myth of "technology transfer" to Africa and the rest of the Third World. This technological retardation has augmented the current crisis by ensuring massive unemployment, due partly to this inappropriate use of capital-intensive technology, and the inability of African countries to afford imported technology and spare parts. Such foreign monopoly of technology ensures the continued lack of skilled labour – including the brain drain caused partly by preference of foreign enterprises, foreign technical assistance (and shamefully, of some African governments) for foreign technical staff to guarantee their continued monopoly of their imported technologies in Africa. The MNCs have also contributed to the displacement of local capital, markets and entrepreneurship. This has been documented not only in Africa but also throughout the rest of the Third World.

1. This was ₦2.6 billion at the exchange rate of around ₦1 = $1.5 during that period.

Table 2.4: Africa: wholesale prices of major export commodities

	Annual % Change			Index: 1980 = 100				
Commodity	1980	1981	1982	1985	1986	1987	1988	1989
Crude Oil	70.3	11.1	−10.7	82.7	40.7	51.6	46.9	58.4
Cocoa	−19.9	−20.1	−16.6	85.0	78.1	75.8	60.8	48.7
Coffee	−11.0	−30.1	5.0	82.4	100.7	69.5	64.6	52.9
Groundnuts	−13.8	28.3	−37.3	72.0	66.9	58.0	58.4	61.3
Cotton	0.4	− 0.9	−18.0	106.8	103.3	105.3	142.3	187.9
Tea	–	–	–	–	–	76.6	80.3	88.1
Phosphates	–	–	–	–	–	88.4	74.4	87.5
Iron Ore	–	–	–	–	–	81.6	84.9	96.4
EEC Commodity Index	–	–	–	83.2	46.3	61.2	52.8	63.5
ECA Commodity Index in Real Terms[1]	–	–	–	–	–	52.8	42.7	50.9

Notes: (1) ECA commodity index deflated by the UN index of the dollar prices of manufactured exports of industrial countries;
(2) The wholesale prices are those quoted on commodity exchange markets in Chicago, London, New York.

Sources: ECA, *Economic Report on Africa,* 1990 p. 27; other ECA data.

Table 2.5 Net resource outflow from Africa ($billion)

Item	1988	1989
1. Net outflow to IMF and World Bank	−1.2	−1.5
2. Capital flight[a]	−2.5	− 2.5
3. Actual debt service payments	−15.9	−17.8
4. Net ODA[b] at current prices and exchange rates	+17.5	+17.5
5. Trade gain/loss on account of terms of trade	−3.7	−1.2
Total net outflow	−5.8	−5.5

Notes: (a) Many estimates of capital flight exceed figure.
(b) ODA = Overseas Development Assistance.

Source: Adedeji, A. (1990) *A Preliminary Assessment of the Performance of the African Economy in 1989 and Prospects for 1990* (ECA; Addis Ababa), p. 22.

The trade liberalization of IMF-World Bank SAPs has been operating in this direction by increasing the grip of foreign capital on African countries through the de-regulation of foreign investment, doctrinaire privatization to foreign capital, etc.

Similarly, the wild currency fluctuations of the 1980s intensified the African crisis in several ways. These include the huge losses on the external reserves of African countries held mostly in dollars, pound sterling and French francs – as the values of these currencies fell, so did the real values of the external reserves of African countries. The fall in the value of these reserves greatly diminished the capacity to pay for essential imports like food, drugs and raw materials. As the availability of these imports fell, so did local production in agriculture, industry and other sectors which they supported. The depletion of external reserves is one of the ways in which Third World countries have been paying for the high living standards of the advanced countries, especially in the US, where huge trade deficits and more than $500 billion in external debt resulted in a record decline of reserve currency value and subsequent depletion of some Third World countries' reserves. the exchange rate fluctuations have also increased the burden of external debt service by African countries. This includes the loss of their external reserves to debt servicing payments and their higher cost in local currency, which imposes inflationary financing or necessitates the printing of additional local money which further contributes to excessive inflation in these countries. Domestic investment has also suffered from these chronic foreign exchange fluctuations due to the acutely increased costs of imported capital, intermediate products, raw materials and spare parts, as well as the uncertain environment for future contractual arrangements. In many cases, entire investment projects have been scrapped simply because sudden exchange rate depreciation or massive generalized devaluation made them unviable.

The inappropriateness of the Western development models foisted on African countries by multilateral institutions and Western scholars or "developmentalists" has also contributed to the crisis. The best examples of such foreign development models are the Polak financial programming model, on which orthodox IMF-World Bank SAPs are based; the so-called two-gap model with a savings gap (investment minus savings) and a trade gap (imports minus exports); the Harrod-Domar model, used for development planning and the ideal-type index approach to modernization, which requires developing countries to replicate or copy the values and institutions of Western societies. The associated policy prescriptions from this Western developmental ideology include export-led growth, import substitution industrialization (ISI), reliance on foreign capital, technology transfer and population control, to mention only a few. (Frank, 1974).

But it has become increasingly apparent that it is not possible to integrate the financial Polak model of the IMF with the Keynesian model of the World Bank into a holistic basis for structural adjustment and growth, let alone for development. Similarly, the two-gap model has a built-in commitment to excessive external dependence and ignores the crucial domestic resource gap, while the Harrod-Domar model focuses on growth rather than development and has the Keynesian short-run orientation. The ideal-typical method is ahistorical and panders to racism in its political and sociological variants. (Amin, 1974).

Correspondingly, the policy prescriptions of these Western models have failed to generate sustained growth, which they confuse with development. While economic growth is narrowly defined in terms of an increase in Gross National or Domestic Product (GNP or GDP), development must include structural transformation and satisfaction of basic needs for the total population, including food, safe drinking water, health care, education, housing, clothing, and transport, redistribution to increase income per head and increased democratic participation. Export-led growth has led to a cul de sac with the collapse of the commodity trade and the excessive import dependence of import substitution industries, leading to current de-industrialization. The external debt crisis arose largely from reliance on foreign capital and technological backwardness has been sustained by the myth of technology transfer rather than indigenous technological development. Human resource development has given way to mere population control, which is necessary but not sufficient for dealing with the elimination of poverty and underdevelopment.

Relative weights of internal and external factors

In debating the relative significance of internal and external factors in the African crisis, the IMF, World Bank and some of their major sponsors and supporters have insisted that internal factors dominate. This is best stated in the words of the World Bank in its LTPS:

> *But the low return on investment is the main reason for Africa's recent decline.* Africa's investment and operating costs are typically 50 to 100 per cent above those in South Asia – the most comparable region (World Bank, LTPS, p.3 emphasis mine).

But this is contradicted by the following disclaimer and statement of nagging doubt in the same publication by the World Bank:

> The experiences of the first generation of Africans after independence raises some searching questions. Does Africa face special structural problems that have not been properly understood? Has the institutional dimension been neglected? have the recent reform programmes been too narrow or too shallow? Could the process of formulating and implementing reforms be improved Has the effect of external factors been correctly assessed? Are external assistance and debt relief appropriate and adequate? More fundamentally, is there a long-term vision that is both credible and energizing? (World Bank LTPS, p. 1).

This quotation shows that the Bank is aware that there are powerful external factors in the crisis such as falling commodity trade and decreasing foreign lending, and that Africa's deep-seated problems – such as socio-economic structures inherited from colonialism – were externally imposed.

But even if we agree that African countries have engaged in large unproductive investment, why did this produce a crisis in the 1980s and not in the 1960s and 1970s? All the internal factors combined did not cause a crisis until the 1980s because the decisive triggers of massive export collapse and deteriorating foreign lending conditions were not there. There is no region in the world, including Europe and North America, that could sustain the export losses and massive increase in external debt servicing foisted on the Third World without falling into crisis. After all, the crisis in the industrialized countries during 1974–78, *The Second Slump* (Mandel, 1980) was caused largely by rising prices of raw materials.

The World Bank's unproductive investment thesis also raises important statistical and structural questions. First, unproductive investment in Africa could not be the cause of the external debt crisis, since the same crisis has existed in other Third World regions where the Bank shows more productive investment. Second, as the Bank itself has repeatedly emphasized, African agriculture is largely a smallholder affair and small cultivators are efficient. So unproductive agricultural investment by the state or government, which is secondary in Africa's agricultural development, could not have caused the region's agrarian crisis – and anti-rural bias is much more than unproductive investment. Third, there are three branches of capital and three main sources of investment in Africa, namely, state or public sector, foreign private capital of the MNCs and private indigenous capital, in that order. Investment in the directly productive economic sectors like agriculture, oil, mining, industry and construction, in addition to banking and commerce, are controlled by foreign and local private capital, and these have been productive – hence the superprofits of the MNCs and the World Bank's penchant for privatization. So how could the subsidiary unproductive investment in these critical sectors generate a sustained massive crisis on the scale of the African crisis since the 1980s? It must be that unproductive public investment played a role in the causation of the crisis, but this role was secondary to that of the collapse and drain of most of the *sources* of investment in African countries, that is export earnings that provide over 80 per cent of total investment resources for the public and private sectors.

For these reasons, we must insist that the World Bank, IMF and their supporters are playing bad politics by insisting on dominant internal causation of the crisis. The motives for their thesis are twofold. One is to deny any special external responsibility for the resolution of the crisis and justify official Western passivity in dealing with it. The suggestion that "African countries caused their crisis, so should clear up the mess they created" seems to be the logic of this false position. In the second place, this bogus thesis suits the detraction of Africa – the "nothing-good-comes-from-Africa" syndrome. These are both patently baseless rationalizations that we must transcend. It is part of the bad politics of adjustment beyond which a more balanced, rational basis for recovery must be predicated. Luckily, economic theory has a relevant prescription here – and this is partly why both the internal and external causes of the crisis have been analysed. The idea is to focus on joint internal and external responsibility for dealing with the crisis – with major African responsibility because, regardless of its cause, the problem is Africa's. Economic theory is very clear on this shared responsibility.

Increasing agreement and shared responsibility

The earlier World Bank quotation on its doubts about the crisis and adjustment in Africa reflects the emerging consensus that crucial external factors have largely generated the crisis and continue to sustain and aggravate it. There is increasing agreement on the futility of blaming the crisis exclusively on internal factors. Africa has always admitted that some of the internal factors identified above have played a role in the emergence of the crisis. Africa has gone beyond this to accept primary responsibility for the resolution of the crisis because the victims of the slump are all in Africa.

The IMF, World Bank and their supporters in the international community should also translate the emerging consensus on the causes of the crisis into practical terms. This requires their corresponding acceptance of shared responsibility for solving the problem, and must transcend any current sentiment of merely "helping" Africa. It demands a moral and political commitment, based on objective analysis and the acceptance of international responsibility. Underlying this should be an enlightened interest in the shared benefits that recovery and development offer to both Africa and to the rest of the world.

The increasing agreement on the domestic and external causes of the crisis must be translated into increasing agreement on policy actions in both Africa and the North for the urgent resolution of the crisis. This need not rest on an agreed joint programme of action, which may be problematic. What is more exigent is that the multilateral financial institutions and the international community implement urgent policy actions in support of African reforms to stem the enormous human and material costs already incurred by adjustment. This has so far been lacking in such critical areas as the revamping of commodity exports, effective external debt relief, more flexible and constructive approaches to adjustment as well as increased financial assistance similar to the $14 billion Bank for Eastern Europe that the OECD countries established in 1990.

Though the multinational financial institutions and their major sponsors maintain that they have been offering substantial assistance for recovery to Africa, its inadequacy is apparent. First, their perception of the crisis as having been caused by Africa has encouraged the pushing of most of the burden of adjustment onto African countries. In the process, Western support to Africa has been grossly inadequate – hence the protraction of the crisis despite Africa's massive adjustment. The Western response has persistently failed to deal decisively with the major external causes as reflected not only by the worsening external debt crisis, but also by the unpopular Frazer report, *Africa's Commodity Problems*. In practical terms, Western assistance has been mere tokenism relative to the magnitude of the crisis and the requirements for its elimination as reflected in the mid-term review of the UN's Programme of Action for African Economic Recovery (UN-PAAERD) in 1988 and in its on-going final evaluation.

The second reason for the inadequacy of external support is its failure to constitute significant *additionality*. Much of the external support for recovery – like the Enhanced Structural Adjustment Facility (ESAF), the Special Programme for Africa (SPA), the Social Dimension of Adjustment (SDA) and the International Commodity Fund (ICF) – have either been used to service foreign debt with little *net* inflow of funds, or been made inaccessible by tough preconditions tied to structural adjustment for drawing such funds, or they have simply supported the expansion of World Bank bureaucracy (as with the SDA, which should have been based in African countries, rather than in the Bank). Thus by mid-1990 most of the ESAF funds had not been disbursed because of conditionality requirements that allowed only 11 countries to gain benefits totalling $1 billion out of the $7 billion in the facility, which ended in November 1990. The ICF is also inaccessible because of conditionality, in addition to being grossly inadequate given the size of the commodity export problem.

In the third place, much of the Western support for Africa's adjustment displaces, rather than supports, Africa's initiatives. The World Bank is the worst culprit here – each time Africa prepares a recovery or development programme, the Bank produces a counter-programme. The Bank prepared its 1981 *Berg Report*[1] to displace Africa's 1980 *Lagos Plan of Action* for its integrative development, and countered the *African Alternative Framework to Structural Adjustment Programmes for Socio-Economic Recovery and Transformation* (AAF-SAP) with its LTPS. Clearly, if some of Africa's development partners see themselves in opposition to the

1. The Berg Report was titled *Towards Accelerated Development in Sub-Saharan Africa* (World Bank, Washington DC), 1981.

region, then not much joint progress can be made towards resolving the current crisis.

But, happily, even economic theory is quite clear on the need for this collaborative international effort for recovery. Theory states that in a situation of crisis, both deficit and surplus countries, or both debtor and creditor countries must adjust together. The deficit/debtor countries should adjust by reducing their imports, increasing exports and reducing consumption and total expenditure. At the same time, the surplus/creditor countries must also adjust by increasing their imports from the deficit countries to increase the export revenue and foreign exchange earnings of the debtor countries, enabling them to repay their foreign debt and eliminate their trade gap. The surplus/creditor countries should also increase domestic spending, foreign aid and external investment making more resources available to the world economy. But the surplus/creditor countries have not been doing these things in relation to Africa. Rather than importing more of Africa's exports, they have mounted export barriers and protectionist policies against Africa and other deficit/debtor regions, while reducing their foreign lending and investment. They then insist that the beleaguered debtor countries should transfer more, rather than less, of their reduced export earnings to the surplus/creditor countries for debt service. It is clear that this is the procedure for making recovery in the deficit/debtor countries very difficult, if not impossible. The adjustment responses of the surplus/creditor countries in the current crisis have thus not conformed consistently with the solution prescribed by economic theory. These responses have pandered more to the politics of a naked power game than to the requirements for optimal functioning of the international economy as an organic whole. Its component parts must adjust according to its inherent logic to sustain the globe as an integrated system. This is the real meaning of increasing global interdependence as an objective reality. This objective *interdependence,* as espoused eloquently by the *Brandt Report,* requires an abiding but subjective global *solidarity.* Although world technology has been increasing global interdependence, it is largely *asymmetrical interdependence* to which developing countries have been losing their relative autonomy. Their dependence on the North has increased and, in the process, they have grown relatively poorer. Like all forms of structural inequality, this growing international inequality is a major source of systemic weakness in the global economy. Rising regional economic blocs in Europe, North America and the Pacific Rim, among the mega-trends to the year 2000, must also be seen correctly as contributing to this alarming trend.

This has become so horrendous as to provoke the World Bank to devote its 1990 Development Report to world poverty. Disturbingly, the study shows that Africa is the only region in the world in which per capita income will be falling right up to the 21st century. This must be appreciated correctly as a major reflection of the current and projected failure of on-going adjustment processes in Africa. Unlike the beleaguered monetary theory followers of the Classical Economists after the Great Depression of 1929-33, we cannot smugly proclaim: "Do not adjust your theory; there is a fault in reality".

In the current crisis, as in the past, reality is objective and it is the duty of both theory and practice to come to grips with it. So far, the theory of mutual and simultaneous adjustment by both deficit/debtor and surplus/creditor countries is valid, unlike the classical theory of automatic full-employment equilibrium that ruled out the possibility of a generalized depression. What is required in the present situation is to realize that there is no fault in reality, and no need for major adjustment to the theory of adjustment. The compelling need is for adjusting the practice of adjustment itself in the surplus/creditor countries. It must always be remembered that the recovery and transformation of Africa will promote the growth and welfare of the entire global economy – as much as it will enhance the prospects for peace and security in the world.

Chapter 3

The politics of the African debt crisis

The crisis is fundamentally political

The popular view of the current debt crisis in Africa, Latin America and South-East Asia (the Third World) is that it is a financial and economic one. This is the conception promoted by the IMF and the World Bank. They insist even that the crisis is the result of the "financial indiscipline" of African leaders. But this is a false diversion. The reality is that the African and Third World debt crisis is also fundamentally a *political* question. It is the result of a historically specific struggle for world resources involving identifiable political forces in the world. The three major political groups involved are:

(a) the so-called creditor group represented by the IMF, World Bank, advanced capitalist countries and imperialist financial institutions – these bodies are cartelized into the Group of Seven, Club of Paris and Club of London;
(b) the so-called debtor group, consisting of African and other Third World governments as well as the masses of the African and Third World countries;
(c) the international community, including the socialist countries and non-governmental organizations (NGOs) in the industrialized capitalist countries. While the crisis is between the (a) and (b) world groups, some unpatriotic elements in the (b) group are in symbiotic alliance with the "creditors", while the international community largely supports the Third World countries.

The debt crisis is fundamentally political in two senses. One is that it represents a basic assault on the hard-won sovereignty of African and other Third World countries. It is a strategy for the recolonization of these countries by world imperialism. The other is that unlike the debt crisis of the 1930s which involved only the Latin American countries, the current debt crisis was not inevitable. At least its catastrophic impact on the poor countries could be avoided but for the non-competitive manipulation of world trade and resource flows by the core capitalist countries. It is this combination of political forces, subversion of sovereignty for recolonization, and imperialist manipulation of global resource flows that underscore the political character of the current debt crisis.

A silent imperialist war of recolonization

Since it started around 1979, the African and Third World debt crisis has unfolded into an act of international aggression and war (George, 1988). The debt war is undeclared and silent so as not to provoke alarm or protests from the media or the public. It is another episode of "silent surrender" – conquest without gun battle. The debt crisis satisfies the motives, mechanisms and effects of conventional war.

The motives are usually to force the adversary to change its course of action, to acquire territory or otherwise to subjugate. The debt crisis has decreased prices of raw materials and silenced demands for a new international economic order, thrown Nigeria and other debtor countries wide open to imperialism, and allowed physical occupation by the IMF and World Bank staff of the Central Banks and Ministries of Finance and Trade of debtor countries.

The standard mechanisms of war are violence and penetration . The debt crisis has led directly and indirectly to thousands of deaths from riots, demonstrations, starvation and epidemics. It has also visited social-psychological violence on millions of unemployed, under-nourished, diseased and demoralized people. The debt crisis has economically penetrated debtor nations, guaranteeing to the imperialists the physical, economic, financial and even ideological forms of the market catechism of structural adjustment; the unbridled capitalism of social Darwinism – the survival of the fittest, by hook or by crook.

The effects of war on the subjugated are manifestly replicated in the current debt crisis. The imperialists are recolonizing our countries and even dumping their nuclear waste on them – a threat of extinction which we did not even face under colonialism. With massive currency devaluation of about one thousand per cent (from ₦1.2 to the pound to ₦11.6 to the pound for travellers' cheques within two years, our raw materials are now virtually free to the imperialists. Other ridiculous local prices to foreigners include a ₦200.00 hotel suite for less than £20 or $30 – the price of a slum hotel room abroad. Import prices are jumping through the roof and there is a huge annual export of capital. The net export of capital from Africa to the IMF in 1986 was $1 billion, and debt rescheduling now costs Africa an extra $1 billion in debt burden annually. Even the Central Bank of Nigeria reported in June 1988 that the outflow of capital from the country has been exceeding the inflow. Instead of old-fashioned military occupation in conventional war, IMF and World Bank staff now occupy the Central Banks and Finance and Trade Ministries of independent African countries, while the multinational corporations have been rapidly extending their grip over African economies through privatization, debt-equity swap, etc. In Mexico, some factories are even being physically relocated to the USA.

Structure and causes of Africa's debt crisis

By December 1987, Africa's total debt stood at $228 billion, about half of that of Latin America and double that of Brazil. Some seventy to eighty per cent of this debt is owed to official creditors, and its burden has been crushing. From $8 billion in 1985, the interest and amortization charges on Africa's debt jumped to $19.5 billion by the end of 1987. The annual *net* payment by Africa to the IMF alone also rose to $1 billion by 1986. Africa has the highest proportion of debt to gross national product (GNP) in the world at 55.1 per cent in 1985. Total debt as a proportion of exported goods and services increased from 167 per cent in 1982 to over 228 per cent by 1987. The *debt service ratio* or total debt service payments as a percentage of annual export earnings which was 15 per cent in 1980 soared to over 50 per cent in 1987 for sub-Saharan Africa, with 62 per cent for Ghana, 67 per cent in Zambia, 84 per cent in Equatorial Guinea and 204.6 per cent in Mozambique. Africa's debts have been growing at the alarming rate of more than 23 per cent annually, which is greater than the growth rate of GDP and of exports.

Equally disturbing is the relation between per capita income and per capita debt shown in Table 3.1.

Table 3.1: Per capita income and external debt in African countries

Country	1984 GNP per capita ($)	1984 Debt per capita ($)
Zambia	470	429
Ivory Coast	620	490
Benin	270	148

Source: ECA, Addis Ababa.

Similarly, while sub-Saharan Africa's growth of GDP per capita was −3.4 per cent during 1980–86, the growth rate of exports of primary goods was a pathetic −2.2 per cent. It has also been projected that by the year 2000, Africa's capacity to import will be less than the 1980 level.

Major causes of the crisis

In addition to the main causes identified above, some critical external factors have been largely responsible for the African and Third World's debt crisis – although IMF and World Bank propaganda blames internal factors in the debtor countries. The basic fact is that the internal factors raised by the Fund and Bank have always been there, but the debt crisis emerged only in the 1980s – due to the profoundly destabilizing impact of the external factors. These external causes of the crisis include the collapse of commodity prices and exports, adverse effects of the crisis in the core capitalist countries, deteriorating foreign loan structure and lending terms, interest rate manipulations (especially by the bankrupt Reagan administration), the exploitative activities of multinationals, the fleecing practices of financial institutions and the untying of foreign loans and exchange rate fluctuations.

Thus the collapse of the prices of cocoa, coffee, tea, copper, bananas and oil products caused foreign exchange losses of $2.2 billion to Africa during 1979–81. According to ECA sources, Africa lost another $13.5 billion during 1980–83 and a staggering $19 billion in one year between 1985 and 1986. The purchasing power of Africa's exports also fell by 25 per cent during 1981–83.

The deterioration of foreign lending terms has also shifted the composition of Africa's debts from concessional official sources to private commercial banks whose share of the debts rose from 32.5 per cent in 1971 to 39.5 per cent by 1980. As debts with variable interest rates increased, the real interest rate on Africa's debt rose from about .7 per cent in 1970 to 1.7 per cent by 1986. The average interest rate on all types of loans to Africa also rose from 4.2 per cent in 1971 to 10.1 per cent by 1982 and higher since. The OAU has estimated that $20.4 billion will be required during 1986–90 to pay rising interest charges on Africa's existing debt.

The extortionate practices of the international banks and other financial institutions have also aggravated Africa's debt crisis. In addition to worsening lending terms, there has also been increased capital export from Africa, rising external controls over capital flows between the continent and the rest of the world, the withholding or

Table 3.2: Developing Africa's external debt ($US)

	1983	1984	1985	1986	1987	1988	1989	1990	% Growth rate 1989	% Growth rate 1990
DEBT STOCKS (EDT)	139,436	143,763	163,950	190,074	220,725	228,246	237,501	243,377	4.1	2.5
Long-term (DOD)	114,645	117,139	135,469	161,392	191,482	199,328	215,394	222,319	8.1	3.2
Official creditors	66,560	70,551	83,142	104,830	123,036	131,905	147,091	154,960	11.5	5.3
Multilateral	18,984	20,000	24,660	31,090	39,614	44,273	50,073	55,503	13.1	10.8
Bilateral	47,576	50,552	58,481	73,741	83,422	87,631	97,018	99,457	10.7	2.5
Private creditors	42,785	40,577	45,661	50,091	61,281	59,630	59,264	57,448	–0.6	–3.1
Private non-guaranteed	5,300	6,011	6,667	6,471	7,168	7,792	9,040	9,912	16.0	9.6
Use of IMF credit	6,061	6,298	7,239	7,587	8,098	7,235	0	0		
Short-term	18,730	20,325	24,242	21,093	21,145	21,682	22,106	21,059	2.0	–4.7
CROSS DISBURSEMENTS	20,482	17,919	16,933	18,269	17,942	20,754	22,357	22,357	7.7	0.8
Long-term	18,663	16,701	15,976	17,359	17,166	19,917	22,357	22,543	12.3	0.8
Official creditors	7,758	7,442	6,894	8,473	9,077	11,992	13,974	14,121	16.5	1.1
Multilateral	3,049	3,259	3,334	4,790	5,322	5,890	8,090	8,679	37.4	7.3
Bilateral	4,709	4,185	3,558	3,682	3,757	6,104	5,884	5,443	–3.6	–7.5
Private creditors	9,327	7,599	7,263	7,142	6,039	6,523	7,092	7,034	8.7	–0.8
Private non-guaranteed	1,578	1,659	1,818	1,744	1,750	1,402	1,293	1,386	–7.8	7.2
IMF purchases	1,819	1,218	956	910	776	837	0	0		

Sources: World Bank, *World Debt Tables*, 1988–89, First Supplement; ECA.

Table 3.3: Developing Africa's foreign debt service payments (units = million $US)

	1983	1984	1985	1986	1987	1988	1989	1990	% Growth rate 1989	1990
PRINCIPAL REPAYMENTS	10,045	10,831	12,421	11,795	11,070	12,345	12,530	14,738	1.5	17.6
Long-term	9,647	10,264	11,630	10,430	9,723	11,048	12,530	14,738	13.4	17.6
Official creditors	1,720	2,170	3,200	3,387	3,565	4,210	5,393	6,133	28.1	13.7
Multilateral	533	767	1,030	1,391	1,723	2,315	2,547	2,386	10.0	–6.3
Bilateral	1,188	1,403	2,170	1,996	1,840	1,894	2,847	3,748	50.3	31.6
Private creditors	7,068	7,223	7,269	5,868	4,856	5,861	6,111	7,699	4.3	26.0
Private non-guaranteed	858	871	1,162	1,174	1,304	978	1,028	905	5.1	–12.0
IMF repurchases	398	567	790	1,366	1,346	0	0			
INTEREST PAYMENTS	7,561	8,635	8,334	8,006	7,482	9,985	10,024	10,866	0.4	8.4
Long-term	5,453	6,062	6,203	6,059	5,878	8,251	8,648	9,514	4.8	10.0
Official creditors	1,496	1,882	2,103	2,509	2,811	4,013	4,590	5,358	14.4	16.7
Multilateral	609	749	841	1,201	1,493	1,909	2,097	2,360	9.8	12.5
Bilateral	887	1,133	1,262	1,307	3,319	2,106	2,492	2,998	18.3	20.3
Private creditors	3,620	3,741	3,687	3,087	2,645	3,762	3,654	3,850	–2.9	5.4
Private non-guaranteed	336	438	414	464	422	476	406	309	–14.7	–23.9
IMF charges	420	481	490	557	400	343	0	0		
Short-term	1,689	2,092	1,642	1,390	1,204	1,391	1,405	1,353	1.0	–3.7

Table 3.3: Developing Africa's foreign debt service payments (Continued)

	1983	1984	1985	1986	1987	1988	1989	1990	% Growth rate 1989	1990
TOTAL DEBT SERVICE (TDS)	17,607	19,464	20,755	19,800	18,553	22,331	22,584	25,603	1.1	13.4
Long-term	15,100	16,326	17,832	16,487	15,604	19,300	21,180	24,252	9.7	14.5
Official creditors	3,217	4,051	5,302	5,895	6,377	8,222	9,983	11,490	21.4	15.1
Multilateral	1,142	1,514	1,872	2,593	3,217	4,223	4,643	4,746	9.9	2.2
Bilateral	2,075	2,537	3,432	3,303	3,158	3,999	5,339	6,745	33.5	26.3
Private creditors	10,689	10,964	10,956	8,955	7,501	9,623	9,764	11,548	1.5	18.3
Private non-guaranteed	1,194	1,309	1,575	1,638	1,726	1,454	1,434	1,214	−1.4	−15.3
Use of IMF credit	816	1,048	1,280	1,922	1,745	1,641	0	0		
NET FLOWS	10,438	7,089	4,512	6,475	6,872	8,409	9,828	7,806	16.9	−20.6
Long-term	9,017	6,437	4,347	6,930	7,443	8,870	9,828	7,806	10.8	−20.6
Official creditors	6,038	5,272	3,694	5,084	5,511	7,784	8,581	7,988	10.2	−6.9
Multilateral	2,517	2,491	2,304	3,398	3,596	3,575	5,542	6,293	55.0	13.6
Bilateral	3,522	2,781	1,389	1,687	1,913	4,209	3,037	1,696	−27.8	−44.2
Private creditors	2,259	376	−5	1,275	1,485	662	981	−665	48.2	−167.8
Private non-guaranteed	720	788	657	570	447	424	266	481	−37.3	80.8
Use of IMF credit	1,421	652	166	−455	−570	−461	0	0		

Table 3.3: Developing Africa's foreign debt service payments (Continued)

	1983	1984	1985	1986	1987	1988	1989	1990	% Growth rate 1989	1990
NET TRANSFERS	2,876	–1,567	–3,822	–1,531	–611	–1,576	–226	–3,062	–85.7	1254.9
Long-term	3,563	375	–1,856	872	1,564	617	1,177	–1,710	90.8	–245.3
Official creditors	4,540	3,391	1,591	2,576	2,700	3,770	3,991	2,631	5.9	–34.1
Multilateral	1,906	1,742	1,462	2,197	2,105	1,666	3,445	3,932	106.8	14.1
Bilateral	2,634	1,648	127	379	594	2,104	546	–1,302	–74.0	–338.5
Private creditors	–1,362	–3,365	–3,691	–1,812	–1,161	–3,099	–2,672	–4,515	–13.8	69.0
Private non-guaranteed	384	351	244	106	25	–52	–141	173	171.2	–222.7
Use of IMF credit	1,003	170	–324	–1,011	–970	–803	0	0	–100.0	ERR
Short-term	–1,689	–2,092	–1,642	–1,390	–1,204	–1,391	–1,405	–1,353	1.0	–3.7
ECONOMIC AGGREGATES										
Exports of G & S (XGS)	70,320	73,119	71,591	61,339	67,007	66,269	76,731	84,708	15.8	10.4
Gross National Product	276,704	278,383	283,627	262,653	252,940	247,751	241,867	248,799	–2.4	2.9

Sources: World Bank *World Debt Tables*, 1988–1989: First Supplement: ECA

selective granting of credit and the adverse review of the creditworthiness of the debtor countries.

The multinational corporations have also been systematically decapitalizing the continent and the rest of the Third World. These MNCs control about 80 per cent of Africa's trade in mineral and agricultural raw materials, and manipulate their prices to impose huge losses on primary producers. Other notorious mechanisms of exploitation by MNCs are the net repatriation of profits of $13.5 billion during 1970–80 (with a net capital export of $2.6 billion from Nigeria during this period), technology rent of $35 billion from the poor countries to the core capitalist countries in 1982 alone, and transfer-pricing, (over-invoicing of imports and under-invoicing of exports).

The untying of foreign exchange fluctuations and loans has also contributed to the debt crisis by allowing the IMF, World Bank and other foreign lenders to facilitate the transfer of these loans into private bank accounts abroad by rogue leaders. This is one major reason why the borrowing countries cannot generate returns on these external loans to repay them. This corrupt "capital flight" into secret Swiss bank accounts was estimated conservatively at $56 billion in 1986. The tying of African currencies to erratically fluctuating imperialist currencies like the dollar has also imposed huge foreign exchange losses on poor countries.

The *internal causes* of the African debt crisis include the systematic looting of the coffers of these countries by some bankrupt leaders, with losses estimated at over $30 billion. Unproductive investment in stadia and other prestige projects, corruptly inflated contracts, anti-rural bias in government programmes, distorted national priorities, chronic budget deficits, official collusion with MNCs and high military spending are also significant factors. During 1978–88, when Africa's arms expenditure was reported to have increased 15 times, African countries squandered about $120 billion for military purposes. It has also been disclosed that Nigeria's financial resources during 1977–82 exceeded the entire amount of money spent on the Marshall Plan for the reconstruction of Western Europe after World War II.

The politics of the African debt crisis is, perhaps, best dramatized by the responses of the major parties to the crisis – the IMF and World Bank on behalf of the creditors, African governments, the African public and the international community.

IMF – World Bank responses to the crisis

The five dominant responses of the Fund and Bank to the African crisis are SAP ideology, co-opting of African governments, use of "fifth columnists" (Payer, 1974), spreading of conditionality and attempts to co-opt foreign NGOs. Even though IMF and World Bank officials know that their countries will not tolerate even 10 per cent of the repressive policies implied by SAP, these harsh and perverse cross-conditionalities are still imposed as a solution to the African debt crisis. They know that these policies have never worked anywhere in the world; they don't even have serious studies of their impact on various countries. But because they are given the power by the debtor countries to impose them, and because SAP satisfies their unstated imperialist objectives, they continue to impose them. In doing so, the IMF and the World Bank are fulfilling their true mission as the stormtroopers of imperialism in its debt war against the Third World.

The second response of the Fund and the Bank to the crisis has been the use of the carrot-and-stick method to encourage collaboration by some African governments in their aggression against Africa. Thus, in spite of the fact that these countries cannot repay their outstanding debt, the Fund and Bank essentially bribe them into taking more loans. Bankrupt African leaders like Mobutu are their heroes, while countries like Zambia and Tanzania, who resist them, are pilloried. Thus at the Abuja Conference in July 1987, the Fund, Bank and their major sponsors essentially goaded African countries into accepting SAP with the false promise of more loans and easy rescheduling. Almost a year later, even the Expanded Special Adjustment Facility (ESAF) and the rhetoric about additional funding are yet to materialize. But the carrot-and-stick game has worked well to stall any vigorous challenge from the OAU.

The third strategy of the Fund and Bank is the use of their "fifth column" of technocrats and other allies in Africa. These are the local lobbies that canvass for the acceptance of pernicious conditionality and SAP. They argue naively that it is the African and other debtors that run to the Fund and Bank after messing up their economies, and that these institutions have imposed nothing. So what conditionality have they imposed on the US - the largest debtor nation, with an external debt of about $650 billion? Between 1945 and 1978 when the creditor countries took over 70 per cent of the total credit of the Fund and Bank, what was the conditionality? And what discipline did the IMF impose on the advanced capitalist countries during the massive monetary disorders of the 1970s? Even the crisis in the African countries has been caused largely by the wrong policies of the Fund and Bank in the past (import substitution industrialization, reliance on foreign capital, etc.) and by the manipulation of the exports of the poor countries. In any case, is it not to deal with disequilibrium and crises that the Fund and Bank were established?

In the fourth place, the IMF and World Bank have been extending the use of conditionality against the debtor countries to other bodies. Thus foreign governments and private foreign creditors now insist on the acceptance of Fund-Bank conditionality as a clearance certificate before even discussing debt rescheduling. Even worse is the alarming fact that the aid component of Lomé III, which terminates in 1990 and which the EEC has boasted about as "aid without strings", has now come under this same conditionality. The ACP (African, Caribbean and Pacific) countries should collectively reject any conditionality imposed on Lomé III or IV.

The fifth response of the IMF and World Bank to the African and Third World's debt crisis has been a recent attempt to co-opt the foreign NGOs that support the creditor countries. The ostensible ploy is to appear to cooperate with the NGOs in giving "adjustment a human face". But African countries must insist on the neutrality of the NGOs. On their part, the NGOs should realize that they will lose their credibility if they become an arm of the Fund and Bank. The EEC does not agree fully with the Fund and Bank but its attachment of conditionality to Lomé III is a disturbing response to the debt crisis. The Toronto summit of the Group of Seven creditor countries showed some marginal flexibility on the debt crisis but this is clearly inadequate.

The response of African governments

As African governments have been perceiving the debt crisis predominantly in financial and economic terms, their responses have been largely individualistic. Each country has been negotiating separately with the Fund, Bank, Club of Paris and Club of London, and trying to repay its debts as a matter of misguided honour. Yet, the enormous power of the IMF and the World Bank derives from their ability to isolate the debtor countries and treat them one by one. On the other hand, the creditor countries have ganged up behind the Fund and Bank as the Group of Seven, Club of Paris and Club of London. Unlike their counterparts in Latin America and Asia, African governments have not been very active in protesting the terms of the debt war.

Only on three occasions have African countries acted collectively on their debt. These are APPER, Abuja and Addis 1987. In July 1985, the OAU adopted Africa's Priority Programme for Economic Recovery (APPER) for 1986–90. It estimated a cost of $128.1 billion for its programme, out of which Africa would provide $82.5 billion and raise the additional $46 billion from external sources. In May 1986 the OAU used APPER to request a special session of the UN to discuss the Critical Economic Situation in Africa. This led to the adoption of the UN Programme of Action for African Economic Recovery and Development, 1986–90 (UN–PAAERD). Unfortunately, this UN programme has merely reinstated the discredited Berg Report[1] prepared by Elliot Berg for the World Bank to undermine the OAU's Lagos Plan of Action for African Integration.

As not much was done to implement UN–PAAERD, the ECA, OAU, ADB (African Development Bank) and Nigerian government jointly organized the Abuja conference in June 1987 as one of the follow-up actions envisaged in UN–PAAERD. The Abuja Statement noted that some 28 African countries were implementing SAPs and the conference ended with OAU members committing themselves to a crippling 30 per cent debt service ratio. APPER, UN–PAAERD and the Abuja Statement all failed because they were *economistic* approaches to the debt crisis.

During November and December 1987, the OAU again convened at Addis Ababa and adopted an African common position on the debt crisis. This was the first real political response to the crisis because it placed common demands on the creditors and called for an international conference on Africa's debt. Its relatively mild demands included the conversion of debts into grants, or their cancellation for the poorest countries (as if there are rich countries in Africa), longer grace and repayment periods on debts, multi-year debt rescheduling, lower interest rates and more bearable debt service ratios. Though some small debts have since been cancelled or converted to grants for some countries, these OAU demands have yet to be accepted.

The response of the African public

Relative to other Third World regions and to Europe, the response of the African public to the debt crisis has been extremely muted to the point of embarrassment. In extreme cases of harsh SAP policies, the public has responded with unstructured violence leading to the death of hundreds of anti-SAP demonstrators across Africa. The worst cases occurred in Zambia, Morocco, Sudan, Sierra Leone and Nigeria. While there have also been sporadic demonstrations and strikes in several countries implementing repressive adjustment programmes,

1. This World Bank report is called *Towards Accelerated Development in Sub-Saharan Africa*.

these have been sporadic and ineffective.

These protests have fallen far short of organized political resistance to the catastrophic impact of the IMF and the World Bank in Africa. There are far fewer NGOs with concrete programmes of mass mobilization in support of African governments against debt than in other parts of the world. The two major exceptions so far are the Institute for African Alternatives (IFAA) and the Organization of African Trade Union Unity (OATUU) based in Accra. Both of these organized two major international conferences in 1987 on the debt crisis and the catastrophic impact of adjustment programmes. Both NGOs expressed strong solidarity with African countries in opposing the aggression spearheaded against them by the IMF and World Bank. They have demanded a political conception of the debt crisis; concerted action by African countries against the Fund and Bank with the formation of an African debtors' cartel to be linked to a Third World debtors' cartel; the withdrawal of IMF/World Bank staff from African Central Banks and Finance Ministries; the conversion of all external debts into grants, their cancellation or collective repudiation; the formulation of alternative national reconstruction programmes to SAP as in Zambia; the elaboration of an alternative development model for Africa based on effective self-reliance; and the formation of broad democratic alliances of workers, peasants, women, students, patriotic intellectuals, churches and mosques to fight against the debt war and to implement these demands. Other African NGOs are gradually waking up to the need for dealing politically with the debt crisis through mass mobilization.

The response of the international community

The international community maintains solidarity with the Third World on the debt crisis. The socialist countries, the European NGOs and the churches regard the debts as unjust and have demanded their cancellation or repudiation and offered material assistance to Third World countries in aid of the vulnerable urban and rural poor. Some of the notable foreign NGOs here are SAREC, FONDAD, trade unions, CRISE, OXFAM, Christian Aid, War on Want, the Quakers, TOES and the World Development Movement. Closer collaboration with African and other Third World NGOs (i.e., southern NGOs) is needed to increase the effectiveness of their humanitarian work and political mobilization against debt. It is important to maintain their independence from the IMF and World Bank. The successful resolution of the debt crisis requires the maintenance and mobilization of this critical political support and interest from the international community in the African crisis – especially at a time when imperialism is rapidly marginalizing Africa in an increasingly hostile international environment.

Towards the resolution of the crisis

The debt crisis of the 1930s was resolved by the massive default by Latin American countries and the subsequent US payment to the private banks involved. But the current debt crisis is different in one major respect – it is an act of silent aggression for the recolonization of Africa and other Third World countries. Hence its overtly political character. Its resolution must, therefore, be fundamentally political. Five factors are critical to this resolution:

1 *Political conception and treatment of debt* – African governments, the African public and their international supporters must think and act on debt in increasingly political terms.
2 *Concerted, collective action* – African governments must shift urgently from narrow individual approaches to collective action on the debt crisis. Negotiating one by one with the Fund, Bank, Club of Paris and Club of Rome is useless. They should insist that the OAU, ECA and ADB negotiate with all African countries on a collective basis. If collective action is good for the strong creditors, it is crucial for the weak debtors. The OAU must urgently form an African debtors' cartel and a Third World debtors' cartel.
3 *Broad Democratic Alliance Against Debt* – All mass organizations of workers (i.e. trade unions), students, women, peasants, patriotic intellectuals, churches and mosques must form broad fronts in each African country. Their purpose must be to support their countries against the catastrophic policies of the IMF and World Bank.
4 *Mass mobilization Against Debt* – The democratic alliance should mobilize public opinion in each African country and on a Pan-African basis against the evils of debt. Lectures, seminars, symposia, workshops and the mass media should be used in different languages to raise popular political awareness of the debt crisis. It is a silent war that is rapidly destroying our countries and our national populations must be mobilized, as in Latin America and Asia, to support our governments against debt.
5 *Democratic Demands on Debt* – The major demands of the broad democratic debt alliance (DED.A.) should include:

- *collective debt repudiation* – it may be disastrous for individual countries to repudiate debt because of imperialist reprisal. But if all or many African and Third World countries repudiate; they can withstand any reprisals. Many reasons justify collective debt repudiation. *Net* export of capital and other resources from Africa and the rest of the Third World, have already repaid these bogus debts. Moreover, *Africa is really a net creditor to world imperialism.* Germany paid reparation to Europe after World War I and to the Jews since World War II for the death of two million Jews. Who has paid reparations to Africa for slavery, colonialism and neocolonialism? These so-called debts cannot cover a fraction of the reparations due to Africa. The choice before Africa and the rest of the Third World is clear enough: disintegration or collective debt repudiation. Africa *cannot* hope to repay these fraudulent debts and survive.

- *adoption of alternative national reconstruction programmes* to the catastrophic SAP imposed by the Fund and Bank. Zambia is gallantly showing this way forward.
- *immediate withdrawal of all IMF/World Bank Staff from African Central Banks and Finance Ministries.*
- *acceptance of an alternative development model* – this must marginalize and trivialize foreign exchange, balance of payments and the foreign trade sector. We need national and collective self-reliance based on meeting the basic needs of the majority of our people for food, water, shelter, clothing, health-care, transport and basic education. We have nobody to enslave and colonize so we cannot develop in the same way as Western Europe, North America and Japan.
- *development of intra-African and South-South trade by barter and serious South-South cooperation* – African and other poor countries will never be able to gain enough foreign exchange to continue their present trade patterns. So they must trade by barter (so-called counter-trade) among themselves. They should also cooperate to produce common sub-regional and regional currencies and drastically whittle down their prostrate external dependence on the advanced capitalist countries – see Report of the South Commission, *Challenge for the South*.
- *reduce all foreign borrowing* – foreign capital has been a mechanism for the de-capitalization of Africa and the rest of the Third World. Much of the foreign loan does not get to Africa and other poor regions. So all foreign borrowing from the IMF, World Bank, etc. should be drastically reduced. If Africa and the rest of the Third World can keep their export earnings and other resources, they will be enough for a more modest development strategy.

Debt repaid and reparations payment to Africa

> If we look at it objectively, Latin America has already paid its debt. But today we still owe more than was originally contracted. Under present conditions the debt can never be paid and will become a kind of "tribute" that Latin America must pay and keep paying for life.

Thus Carlos Perez de Castillo, Secretary-General of SELA which represents 26 Latin American and Caribbean countries echoed the fact that the Third World countries have already repaid their external debts. The major factors that show that the debt has been paid include high and rising interest rates; falling export earnings; capital flight and profit repatriation by MNCs. (Adedeji, 1990, pp. 99–100). Two ideas have been proposed to counteract the effects of high interest rates. One is that the foreign loans retaining legitimacy should be those given for development purposes at concessional rates – plus short-term export or trade credits. The other is that the only legitimate interest rates on commercial loans should be those charged at real rates, i.e. nominal or money interest rates adjusted for price changes or inflation – and these real interest rates should be near the historical average of 1 to 1.5 per cent. *GATT-Fly*, a Canadian-based ecumenical coalition for economic justice, has thus calculated that in 1986 the interest rates should have been adjusted downward; that in four of the seven years from 1981 to 1987, the legitimate real rates were negative – implying that foreign creditors should have been making payments to debtor countries rather than extracting payments from them. Instead, the real interest rates paid on commercial loans averaged a whopping 15.2 per cent during 1981–87 – an excess of 13.7 per cent above the historical norm of 1.5 per cent! When this excess real interest rate of 13.7 per cent is applied to Africa's total debt of $230 billion in 1987, the *excess interest payment* alone by Africa between 1981 and 1990 comes to over $32 billion. These excessive interest charges are the source of the perversion ensuring that after countries have made repayments of about 75 per cent of the principal on a loan, the unpaid balance usually exceeds the total amount of the original loan – due to interest rate manipulations.

On reduced export earnings, the ECA has calculated that low commodity prices have cost Africa $54.3 billion in lost export earnings between 1981 and 1987 or up to $60 billion by 1990. This also represents a transfer from Africa to the creditor countries. According to IMF estimates, about $30 billion of capital flight was hauled out of Africa between 1974 and 1985 or $42.5 billion by 1990 as a low variant.

The figure has been much higher since then, and due to the huge amount involved, Africa's foreign debt should be discounted by the same amount. It has also been estimated that about $75 billion of Africa's $243.4 billion foreign debt in 1990 was due to high interest rates and losses from fluctuations in the exchange rates of the US dollar. The export of capital from Africa by the MNCs from 1974–90 (shown as "investment income" in the balance of payments), can also be estimated at around 25 per cent of annual private foreign capital inflows of about $4 billion plus transfer pricing, a total of $25 billion at a rate of 1.5 billion annually.

The total resource outflows from these four sources alone from 1974–90 are shown in Table 3.4.

Table 3.4: Four other sources of external debt repayment by Africa

Loss of export earnings	$77.7 billion
Capital flight	$42.5 billion
High interest rates plus dollar depreciation	$75.0 billion
Capital export by MNCs	$25.0 billion
Total	$220.2 billion

Deducted from Africa's total foreign debts of $243.4 billion in 1990, this figure reduces Africa's outstanding external debts to only $23.2 billion. With the usual 10 per cent of the total debt or $24.3 billion allowed for errors of omission due to lack of documentation, the entire debt is invalidated[1] and it becomes clear that Africa has more than repaid all of its external debts.

Africa's demand for reparations payments

In addition to calling for acceptance of the objective facts that Africa's external debt, and that of the rest of the Third World, has thus been over-paid, Africa is demanding reparations payment from the foreign creditors. This would be compensation or restitution for four centuries of slavery from 1451 to 1883, 100 years of colonialism and 30 years of recolonial depredations. The demand was tabled internationally at the

1. During 1988–89, Nigeria's total external debt was disputed between the governments estimate of around $18 billion and the World Bank calculation of $24 billion. Such discrepancies are common in other countries.

joint *Africa-America Reparations Conference* held in Lagos, December 13–14 1990.

The demand for urgent reparations payment to Africa is motivated by several factors. First, reparations payments have been made, and are still being made, to other regions and groups in Europe and Asia. After World War I, the Allied Powers forced Germany to make reparations payments for war damages to the rest of Europe. The effects of these payments on the balance of payments of both the paying and receiving countries, Germany and the rest of Europe, respectively, have since become a standard topic in the theory of the balance of payments, or financial aspects of international trade. At the end of the Second World War, West Germany was also made to pay reparations for the death of two million Jews in the holocaust. The Japanese victims of the atomic bomb holocaust in Hiroshima and Nagasaki have also received reparations payment from the USA.

Africa lost an estimated 30 million people during the Atlantic Slave Trade in addition to enduring horrendous destruction of property, infrastructures and cultures in slave raids and the disruption of economic activities for eight long generations (Williams, 1972 and Rodney, 1970). During colonialism, Africa again lost millions of people in colonial wars and massacres, or so-called "punitive expeditions", and suffered massive destruction of fledgling infrastructures, production systems, property and vibrant cultures. Economic activities were impossible for long periods and the imposed colonial economic system was the harbinger of the abusive under-development and the horrendous socio-economic scars that Africa bears to this day (Rodney, 1972; Onimode, 1988). After flag independence (because Africa has yet to decolonize effectively, especially in the economic sphere), multilateral imperialism unleashed the multinational corporations for the continued super-exploitation of African countries in a new *form*. In the process, the region's resources have been looted across the continent, and the inherited but distorted colonial structures of disarticulation have been intensified. If the Germans have paid billions of dollars to the rest of Europe and to the Jews, and the US has paid billions to the Japanese, then trillions of dollars are certainly due to Africa and peoples of African descent in the Diaspora (US, Caribbean and Latin America).

The immorality and outrage inspired by the external debt crisis, the imposition of debt peonage on Africa and the emasculation of the fragile sovereignty of its countries cry out for urgent redress. The quick cartelization of the credit countries and their clear manipulation of debt and adjustment to implement a political programme of recolonization demand a straightening of international records. When reviewed objectively, the evidence shows clearly that Africa is a net creditor to the international economy. The reparations payment due to Africa from the West runs into trillions of dollars compared to the so-called foreign debt that Africa is alleged to owe. Any system of morality that requires Africa to have paid billions of dollars annually to the same countries that programmed it into abject poverty must also compel the urgent payment of reparations to Africa for the terrible damages inflicted on it through centuries of mindless super-exploitation and pillage. An International Committee has been established to collect and collate the evidence before making a formal presentation to the 1991 Summit of OAU Heads of State and Government in Abuja, Nigeria. From there, the issue should go to the appropriate international forum for implementation.

But there are those who raise practical doubts over reparations payments to Africa. They argue that previous reparations payments were based on power inequality, in which one party compelled the other to pay. So Germans were forced to pay the rest of Europe and the Jews. Thereafter, this argument is flawed because the Japanese were defeated in World War II and had no political power to compel the Americans to pay – yet they have been paying. So the case that Africa has no political power to enforce such reparations payments cannot hold on the basis of precedent. This is not to suggest, however, that political power is not a factor in the payment of reparations. It is, and that is why Africa is taking concerted political action at the level of the OAU and will back this support – from Third World countries in the context of the Non-Aligned Movement and South-South cooperation, from the UN system, and from the NGOs of the North and South as well as the rest of the international community. If it becomes necessary, recourse can also be had in the International Court of Justice. At the very minimum, Africa must table its demand for reparations payment against the Western demand for debt payment so that, henceforth, the negotiations have to weigh their debt against our debt. The whole world must know that world capitalism is a net debtor to Africa and that Africa is a net creditor to international capitalism. The necessary political will and self-confidence must be mobilized to press this historical demand and effect reparations payments to Africa before African countries collapse completely.

Chapter 4

The debate over adjustment

The scope of the debate

The debate over adjustment in Africa and the rest of the Third World spanned the 1980s and is still raging. It involves various rationalizations and reactions to the different programmes that have been formulated and implemented to deal with the foreign debt problems together with the general socio-economic crisis in Africa, Latin America and Asia.

The main parties to the adjustment debate are the IMF, World Bank, their major sponsors or international creditor countries and other supporters, on the one hand, and the adjusting countries and their supporters in the international community on the other hand. So just as the protagonists of orthodox adjustment among the Bretton Woods institutions (IMF and World Bank) have supporters in the North and South (including supporters in the adjusting countries who are beneficiaries of the adjustment process), the antagonists also draw supporters and sympathizers from the North and South, especially among the NGOs. Hence it is neither correct to see the adjustment debate as a North–South divide, nor to regard the United Nations Economic Commission for Africa (ECA) as the only or main opponent of orthodox adjustment as the IMF and World Bank do.

The adjustment debate has been carried out at three main levels:

- Between the adjusting African countries and their supporters (especially the non-governmental organizations – NGOs) in the South and North, and the IMF, World Bank and creditor countries. This level of the debate has been asymmetrical and unbalanced because, while the Fund and Bank represent all the creditor countries in the Paris Club and London Club and negotiate collectively, African countries have been obliged to negotiate individually most of the time. The main occasions when African countries acted or negotiated collectively were in 1986 on the *African Priority Programme for Economic Recovery* (APPER) which was adopted by the UN General Assembly as the *UN Programme of Action for African Economic Recovery and Development* (UN-PAAERD), *Africa's Common Position on*

External Debt in 1987 and since 1989 on the *African Alternative Framework to Structural Adjustment Programmes for Socio-Economic Recovery and Transformation* (AAF-SAP). This unbalanced approach has been due to the refusal of the Fund and Bank to deal with African countries as a group. The pretext has been that African countries have usually applied for loans to the Fund and Bank individually, so their stabilization and adjustment programmes have to be handled on a country-by-country basis;

- At the level of the international community, between the adjusting African countries and their supporters and sympathizers in the North and South, especially among the NGOs, the World Council of Churches and some members of the UN system, on one hand, and the IMF, World Bank, the creditor countries and their supporters, on the other;
- Within individual adjusting African countries between beneficiaries and losers – between government officials and their supporters, especially among the organized business community or Chambers of Commerce, multinational corporations (MNCs) "fifth columnists" and other beneficiaries of orthodox adjustment programmes, on one hand, and the mass of the population that are victims of orthodox adjustment such as workers, students, women, peasants and members of the middle class such as academics and economists, on the other.

In the course of the adjustment debate, it has been typical to find supporters of orthodox adjustment at all three levels teaming up together, while the opponents at all three levels have also been teaming up. Thus in international conferences on the subject, representatives of the IMF, World Bank, creditor countries and their supporters usually defend the stabilization and adjustment programmes, while representatives of adjusting countries and most NGOs in the South and North oppose them. But in most national conferences, government officials, representatives of the Fund and Bank and their supporters usually team up against the domestic and international opponents of orthodox adjustment.

As used here, adjustment covers the following four broad programmes:

1 National Recovery or Stabilization Programmes in African and other countries which were formulated as the domestic response to the crisis;
2 IMF Stabilization Programmes such as the Stand-by Arrangement (SBA) and the Extended Fund Facility (EFF) which involve "conditionalities";

3 IMF-World Bank Structural Adjustment Programmes (SAPs) or Economic Recovery Programmes (ERPs) as SAPs are called in Ghana, Tanzania and some other countries – these SAPs/ERPs were preceded by World Bank/IMF Sectoral Adjustment Loans (SECALs) – conditionalities are also attached to these SAPs/ERPs and SECALs;
4 The *African Alternative Framework to Structural Adjustment Programmes for Socio-Economic Recovery and Transformation* (AAF-SAP) or simply the *African Alternative* which was launched in July 1989, drawn by the ECA and endorsed by the OAU, UN General Assembly and the Non-Aligned Movement.

National Recovery Programmes

Several African countries like Nigeria, Uganda, Guinea (Conakry), etc. had National Recovery Programmes for dealing with the crisis, which were at various stages of implementation when the IMF replaced them with its Stabilization Programmes. This gave the false impression that the national programmes had failed or were ineffective, but the facts were that these national programmes were not given external support and thus could not cope simultaneously with national recovery and external debt repayment, which has been the priority of the IMF and World Bank in the crisis. So when the adjusting African countries approached the IMF for accommodation with respect to their external debt service and balance of payments deficit/crisis, the Fund insisted on their adoption of its stabilization programmes in place of the extant national programmes, and imposed stiff conditionalities on the stabilizations programmes.

For example, Nigeria was implementing a comprehensive programme of National Economic Emergency form 1985 in addition to an Economic Stabilization (Temporary Provisions) Act of 1982, which was extended twice during 1983–84 and 1985, when the Fund demanded the implementation of its own stabilization programme with tough conditionalities as a requirement for a two billion dollar loan. The IMF loan and its conditionalities, especially currency devaluation, trade liberalization and removal of petroleum subsidy, were put to a national debate. The public returned a stunning NO verdict against them and the IMF loan. But though the IMF loan and its stabilization programme were not adopted formally, the country was forced to replace its national recovery programmes with an IMF-World Bank Structural Adjustment Programme (SAP) from July 1986 to June 1988, and this SAP has been extended since then.

IMF programmes

The controversial features of the IMF stabilization programmes or Stand-by Arrangements are first, their tough conditionalities, called "IMF medicine" or "pill". These include massive devaluation, trade liberalization, removal of subsidies across-the-board, drastic budget cuts and a deflationary credit squeeze, reliance on market forces for getting prices right, doctrinaire privatization of public enterprises, increased interest rates and massive retrenchment. Second is the insistence on financial stabilization – restoration of balance of payments equilibrium, budget balance, price stability and credit balance before the resumption of growth. Last is the one-to-two-year duration of the stabilization programmes which are limited to the external trade and financial sectors (Payer, 1974).

As the Fund's stabilization programmes failed to achieve even limited financial stability without growth and provoked "IMF riots" and stiff opposition, they were replaced by the World Bank's 1980 introduction of Sectoral Adjustment Loans (SECALs) in Kenya and other countries. Some of these SECALs were sponsored by the Bank alone and others were supported by the Bank and Fund, as in Liberia and Sierra Leone. By the mid-eighties, the SECALs were expanded into full Structural Adjustment Programmes (SAPs) or Economic Recovery Programmes (ERPs), especially from 1986. These are comprehensive programmes for overall national economic management that go beyond the Bank's traditional anti-poverty and infrastructural programmes as well as beyond the Fund's usual trade and financial preoccupations. They are supervised jointly by the Fund and Bank with each institution contributing a separate model (the Fund uses Polak's financial programming model and the Bank uses the Keynesian two or three-gap model), (World Bank 1989). Thus these SAPs/ERPs have the three controversial features of Fund stabilization programmes with the following additions and modifications:

(a) they profess some concern for growth but implicitly insist on financial stabilization before the resumption of economic growth;
(b) they are more comprehensive and embrace sectoral reform programmes/policies for finance, agriculture, industry, etc.;
(c) their time frame is the medium-term of an average of two to three years with longer duration in some cases;
(d) the ideological commitment is more explicit in these SAPs/ERPs with respect to the promotion of unfettered or *laissez-faire* capitalism under the slogan of liberalization and the reduction of the role of the state;
(e) their conditionalities have been extended beyond the London

Club and Paris Club of creditors and the individual creditor countries to Lome IV (the trade agreement between the European Community and the African, Caribbean and Pacific (ACP) countries) and other external financing for Africa and other areas; and

(f) these SAPs/ERPs have become the new Western development model being foisted on Africa.

From these features, the adjustment debate has focused mainly on three areas: conceptualization and sponsorship; conditionalities and policies and the impact of adjustment programmes ranging from national to Fund and Bank programmes.

Conceptualization and sponsorship

The adjustment controversies around the broad question of conceptualization and sponsorship have been essentially fivefold:

- who should formulate adjustment policies and programmes;
- the sequence of stabilization and growth;
- the norm of the adjustment process;
- ideology and paradigm; and
- the relationship between orthodox adjustment and the transformation of African economies.

Sponsorship

While there has been broad agreement that all economies and systems must adjust, especially to major shocks like the African crisis, there has been sharp disagreement over who should initiate and formulate the adjustment policies and programmes. The African and Third World position is that this should be the adjusting countries themselves – with the technical assistance and material support of the Bretton Woods institutions. This is to preserve the priorities of the adjusting countries and their sovereignty over national economic management. But while the Bank states in its rhetoric that it maintains this position, both the Fund and Bank do the exact opposite – they replace national recovery programmes with their own stabilization and SAPs on a take-it-or-leave-it basis. This is clear from their despatch of the so-called Policy Framework Paper (PFP) from Washington to the African countries. Indeed, even when countries like Burkina Faso, with healthy balance of payments and external reserves, do not need a structural adjustment programme (SAP), the Bank insisted in 1990 that they must have a SAP as a condition for external financial assistance from any Western source. And when such countries produced their own home-grown SAPs and sent them to the IMF and World Bank, they have been set aside and a Fund-Bank SAP imposed. This shows that the Fund and Bank are using SAP as a political instrument of control in their unstated assignment of constructing a world capitalist system in which trade and private capital can circulate without hindrance. This is also why the objectives of orthodox stabilization and SAPs conflict so sharply with the articulated long-term development objectives of African countries.

Stabilization before growth?

Though nobody denies the desirability and even necessity for financial stabilization in the growth process, the question is the sequence in which these should be pursued. The Fund and Bank insist that African countries should first stabilize before resuming economic growth. This is despite the fact that the achievement of financial stabilization has remained elusive for over a decade. Money is a veil in economics and the financial imbalances of the debtor countries are largely a result of their underdevelopment and lack of rapid economic growth, rather than vice versa. Thus balance of payments disequilibrium and inadequate government revenue are largely the consequence of the slow growth of exports and overall production as well as the structural rigidities of these countries. So it is virtually impossible to achieve financial balances in these countries before their structural bottlenecks that pre-empt growth and development have been drastically reduced. Hence the insistence of African countries and their supporters that stabilization and adjustment, economic growth and transformation must be pursued simultaneously for maximum effectiveness. Africa is in too much of a hurry to eliminate its grinding poverty and arrest its growing marginalization to keep its growth and transformation on hold while pursuing a myopic programme of financial stabilization alone. This is merely a ploy for keeping Africa backward and marginalized, and it is, therefore, politically unacceptable.

Norm of adjustment

There has also been intense controversy over the norm or standard of adjustment in Africa. To what norm should African economies adjust, and what variables and parameters should be adjusted? The answer of the Fund and Bank is that the norm of adjustment should be financial and that it is financial variables like balance of payments, external reserves, budgets, market prices and subsidies that should be adjusted. But this ignores the fact that these financial variables are a veil that reflect the underlying real structures of production, consumption, technology, trade, income distribution and power in any country. These are the structures of disarticulation that generated and continue to sustain and aggravate the African crisis. This is why the crisis is fundamentally a long-term *structural* crisis, rather than a Keynesian problem of insufficient demand. The evidence in African countries is of inadequate productive capacity to meet demand, and this is the basic cause of the chronic shortages that contribute to excessive inflation. Hence the norm of adjustment must be the real structures which sustain the financial imbalances – unless these structures change, there is not much prospect of achieving durable financial stability.

Ideology and paradigm of stabilization and SAPs

The IMF, World Bank and their supporters are very fond of presenting their stabilization and SAPs as neutral, technical and objective sets of policies devoid of significant political and ideological interests, objectives or preferences. This is, perhaps, the greatest subterfuge in the politics of adjustment – which is designed precisely to conceal the true character of stabilization and SAPs. Thus the Bretton Woods institutions are clearly ideological institutions – before their role as financial institutions. This is because their major sponsors are core capitalist countries; their implicit common mandate is the ideological task of constructing and maintaining a world capitalist system (whether good or bad); their journals – *IMF Staff Papers* and *Finance and Development* espouse capitalist ideology; and their training programmes are also deeply steeped in capitalist ideology. This is why Fund–Bank stabilization and SAPs have an economic and political ideology. The economic ideology is liberal or *laissez-faire* capitalism, while the political ideology is anti-statism and political repression.

In contrast to these extremist, rightist ideologies, African countries have been pursuing and remain committed to such other ideologies as scientific socialism, African socialism and mixed economy or welfare statism. They maintain, quite rightly, that the choice of a national ideology is an integral expression of national sovereignty. Hence it is inconsistent for the IMF and World Bank to proclaim ritual respect for the sovereignty and support of the African countries, while simultaneously imposing reactionary economic and political ideologies on them through stabilization and SAPs. This affront to the sovereign right of African countries to choose their own path of national development has been strongly opposed in the adjustment debate, especially within individual countries.

The paradigm or conception of reality in IMF–World Bank stabilization and adjustment programmes has also been hotly contested. This paradigm is a mixed grill of classical, neoclassical and Keynesian paradigms, and it flows from the ideology of the Fund and Bank. The most important element of this paradigm is the obsession with "things" and commodities rather than people – things like prices, capital, money, credit, investment, commodity exports and imports and GDP. This paradigm borrows its commitment to free market forces or *laissez-faire* reliance on the "invisible hand" to run the economy, minimum government, and gradual change from Classical economics; mixes these with its focus on "things" or commodities and equilibrium (balance or stabilization) from neoclassical economics; and lumps all these together with demand management and GDP/GNP focus borrowed from Keynesian economics. The result is a thorough hotchpotch of conflicting conceptions and misplaced commitments that are inappropriate for developing countries. Thus Classical free market forces, minimum government and gradualism as well as neoclassical preoccupation with commodities and focus on equilibrium are all outdated by more than one hundred years since the rise of the welfare state. Demand management is equally misplaced in developing countries whose basic problem is supply shortage due to low productive capacity.

Orthodox adjustment or transformation?

The conceptual debate also involves the conflict between IMF–World Bank orthodox stabilization and SAPs, and the structural transformation required and demanded in Africa. There are three basic issues here. First, that orthodox adjustment keeps growth and transformation on hold – stabilize and adjust first before worrying about transformation or development, despite an elusive ten year chase down this route. Second, orthodox adjustment ignores or cannot deal with the root causes of underdevelopment and lack of transformation in Africa. This is because it sees the African crisis as a short-term and largely financial problem, rather than the long-term structural problem that it is. Hence Fund–Bank orthodox adjustment does not, and cannot, grapple with the structural barriers to transformation such as excessive external dependence, low technology, poor development and utilization of human resources, the domestic resource gap and perverse consumption. Third, orthodox adjustment even blocks the possibility of transformation by generating additional barriers to development, through the destruction of human resources by massive brain drain, growing unemployment and illiteracy, falling enrolment, collapse of education, health, the welfare state and of institutions; de-industrialization from factory closures; displacement of local production by import liberalization; excessive inflation from massive currency destruction through huge devaluation; net transfer of resources from Africa with over one billion annually to the IMF and World Bank; increased external dependence; the undermining of African cooperation through the atomistic or country-by-country approach of orthodox stabilization and SAPs; the strategic weakening of the state in Africa; and the undermining of the democratization process through the high-handed bureaucratic and elitist approach of SAPs. In these different ways, orthodox adjustment is adamantly incompatible with the sustained structural transformation or development of African economies.

Debate over adjustment conditionalities and policies

The most hotly and widely debated aspects of IMF and World Bank stabilization and SAPs are their conditionalities, cross-conditionalities and policy packages. These preconditions which must be satisfied to get Fund–Bank loans for stabilization and SAPs are part of the policies that are implemented under these programmes. These cross-conditionalities and policies are usually given in the Policy Framework Paper (PFP) and elaborated in the actual adjustment programmes. Borrowing countries have to accept or agree to implement these tough conditions before they can be granted loans or facilities under the Extended Fund Facility (EFF), Stand-by Arrangement (SBA) of the IMF, the Sectoral Adjustment Loans (SECALs), Structural Adjustment Loan (SAL) or the Enhanced Structural Adjustment Facility (ESAF) of the IMF and World Bank. When borrowing countries accept these conditionalities, begin drawing from the loans, then fail to implement them fully or violate them, the stabilization or adjustment programmes are cancelled and the loans are stopped – and this often happens several times in one country.

These conditionalities and cross-conditionalities are (Payer, 1974):

- generalised currency devaluation of 30 per cent to 60 per cent and over 400 per cent in one year (with about 900 per cent *de facto* devaluation in some countries);

- massive retrenchment of 20 per cent and more of the workforce, without compensation or redeployment;
- drastic budget cuts and credit squeeze with the withdrawal of subsidies from various activities, services and sectors or across-the-board;
- liberalization of imports and exports with the abolition of exchange control;
- doctrinaire privatization of public enterprises or parastatals, including profitable ones;
- price deregulation for "getting prices right" with reliance on free market forces and abolition of price control as well as controls on other prices like exchange rates, interest rates, wages, rent, etc;
- raising interest rates to get positive real rates of interest.[1]

More recently, some have called for a political conditionality so that governments that deny multi-party democracy and basic human rights would be denied foreign aid. The Fund, Bank other multilateral financial institutions and creditor countries have not formally agreed to impose this additional conditionality, but it has been used in some cases, for instance against Kenya, Zaire, Liberia under Doe, etc.

The debate over these conditionalities has focused on their selective country targets, uniform application, severity and inappropriateness as economic remedies for crisis. Thus it has been observed that these conditionalities have been targeted at the developing countries alone because they were not applied to the advanced countries that took about 70 per cent of IMF facilities between 1944 and 1978.

In the profound monetary disorders of the 1970s in the Western countries, the IMF applied no real discipline. So Fund-Bank discipline and conditionalities are partisan and biased against the weak developing countries. It is for the same reason that the USA, also a debtor country with an external debt (more than twice that of the whole of Africa), is not subjected to conditionalities, stabilization or SAP.

The IMF – and the World Bank – have also been likened to bad doctors who prescribe the same cure for all ailments to all patients. Regardless of the causes and symptoms of balance of payments problems and socio-economic crisis in the Third World, countries are

1. The real rate of interest is the inflation adjusted interest rate. It is equal to the nominal or money rate of interest minus the rate of inflation, i.e.,

$r = i - \frac{\triangle P}{P}$, where r = real rate of interest;

i = nominal or money rate of interest; $\frac{\triangle P}{P}$ = rate of inflation.

forced to devalue, remove subsidies and apply deflationary measures – despite empirical evidence that these policies have rarely worked to resolve crisis in any country. Thus in Africa, Ghana has been under the cure of the IMF since Nkrumah was overthrown in 1966 and is still adjusting under the Fund and Bank – after a quarter of a century!

The harsh character of these conditionalities has also been widely decried. They are so tough that few regimes, whether military or elected, have ever had the courage to implement them fully. And where they are implemented at all, this typically requires the imposition of authoritarian regimes – often through the militarization of politics, the overthrow of elected civilian governments and the scandalous undermining of democracy. The conditionalities are also harsh in terms of their actual or expected effects on people and the economy: massive unemployment from retrenchment, inflation after devaluation or social services crisis after subsidy withdrawal. And most of these effects tend to aggravate the initial problems of countries implementing the conditionalities.

This is partly because the conditionalities are wrong or inappropriate from the point of view of economic theory. It is wrong, for example, to liberalize imports (rather than restrict them) in order to remove balance of payments deficit or disequilibrium, and also wrong to raise interest rates (instead of lowering them) as a cure for depression. Devaluation is also a last resort, not a first option, for dealing with external payments problems – and high rates of devaluation of over 50 per cent are not encouraged because of their disruptive effects. Drastic budget and credit squeeze is also deflationary and worsens unemployment. Reliance on free market pricing in a context of structural rigidities and poor supply response is ill-advised as is doctrinaire privatization rather than selective commercialization with the pragmatic use of the public and private sectors. For similar reasons, massive retrenchment imposes incredible human suffering and is politically unacceptable. Political conditionality has also been opposed because even though it may promote democratization in some cases, it is an affront to national sovereignty, an excuse for interfering in the internal affairs of countries, and a partisan instrument for destabilizing unfavoured governments whose leaders disagree with creditor countries.

Adjustment policies

Though these conditionalities are being implemented as adjustment policies in some 34 African countries that have adopted SAPs, they are only part of adjustment policy packages. In addition, adjustment policies include adjustment objectives, their demand management approach, time frame and other specific policies. The objectives of orthodox adjustment policies, are usually defined by the IMF and World Bank to achieve balance of payments equilibrium, get prices right, balance budgets or eliminate budget deficits (i.e., stop large deficit financing), control inflation or promote stable prices and expand exports. In Nigeria, the objectives of SAP also include the integration of the country more firmly into the world capitalist system (Nigeria, SAP, 1986). These objectives then become the "*performance criteria*" of SAPs. While these goals are desirable, critics argue that they are not the objectives set by African countries for themselves, which have been elaborated in the *Lagos Plan of Action* (LPA) since 1980. (OAU, 1981). These long-term development objectives are:

- achievement of regional food self-sufficiency through domestic food production – not just food security that can be achieved through volatile food aid and food imports;
- satisfaction of critical needs for food, safe drinking water, clothing, housing, health care, education and transport;
- elimination or alleviation of poverty; and
- achievement of effective regional integration through national and collective self-reliance. The SAP objectives divert attention from these goals.

The demand management approach and focus of orthodox adjustment policies has also been controversial. The IMF and World Bank argue that excessive deficit financing, over-expansion of credit and high inflation are bad for recovery and should be eliminated through the use of Keynesian demand management policies. These include drastic budget and credit squeeze, elimination of subsidies, high interest rates, sharp increases in user charges for utilities, higher market prices and massive generalized devaluation. But critics maintain that the monetarist demand management orientation of SAP policies is a reflection of defective analysis and wrong conceptualization of the African crisis by the Fund and Bank. The basic problem in the crisis is low productive capacity of supply shortages – it is because supply is drastically inadequate that demand seems excessive. Indeed, even the large budget deficits or deficit financing in African countries is the consequence of shortages of revenue, foreign exchange earnings and of domestic production due to low tax base, falling export volumes and prices as well as low technology and productivity in domestic production activities. Moreover, Fund–Bank demand management is typically deflationary and operates to aggravate rather than improve the domestic supply situation. Thus high interest rates of around 35 per cent in many countries operating SAPs penalize investment and discourage domestic production while subsidy in agriculture does the same. The Western countries use these agricultural subsidies to produce their surplus food stuffs, which they dump on Africa, undermining domestic agricultural production. Drastic budget and credit cuts across the board also reduce investment spending and discourage domestic production, while massive generalized and frequent devaluations have made it very difficult to plan and implement investment projects with import content.

The short-term time frame of orthodox stabilization and adjustment programmes has also featured in the adjustment debate. Most of these orthodox Fund–Bank programmes are initially for one or two years – even where they are repeated for five or more years in succession. In some countries, some of these programmes are suspended or terminated after six months and replaced by another one-year programme. This is based on the wrong conceptualization of the African crisis as a short-term Keynesian recession that requires mere pump-priming or fine-tuning over a year or two. As a result, these quick-fix Fund–Bank programmes have become major sources of instability and frequent change in the adjusting countries. Their bureaucracies are severely destabilized and always preparing for one programme projects, missions, reports or appraisal in a manner that builds discontinuity and a permanent sense of crisis management or fire-fighting which is unsuitable for a consistent policy of recovery with transformation. In the process, orthodox adjustment distorts and loses sight of the fundamentally long-term structural nature of the African crisis.

In addition to all these, other policies in the orthodox stabilization and adjustment programmes have been controversial. These include the search for positive real interest rates through high nominal interest rates in order to increase savings, the drastic withdrawal of subsidies across the board, the pin-point targeting of policy measures, the country-by-country application of adjustment policies and the tendency towards de-industrialization in adjustment programmes. Though the Fund and Bank decry negative real interest rates in African countries due to high inflation and low nominal interest rates,[1]

---

1. For example, if the nominal or money interest rate is 12% and the annual rate of inflation is 20%, the real interest rate will be –8.0%, i.e.,
real interest rate $r = i - \frac{\Delta P}{P} = 12 - 20 = -8\%$, where i = nominal interest rate,
$\frac{\Delta P}{P}$ = annual rate of inflation.

they accept the same negative real interest rates in Latin America and even in the USA in 1978 and other years. Thus with over 2000 per cent annual rate of inflation in Latin American countries, it is clear that no feasible nominal interest rate will yield a positive real interest rate.

But this is not to deny the undesirability of negative real interest rates. Moreover, to get positive real interest rates, it is better to hold down the rate of inflation than to raise the nominal interest rate too high and discourage investment. It is also not true that savings depend on the real interest rate – this is the classical theory of savings that is out-dated by over a hundred years. Even empirical results in several countries show that the relationship between savings and the real interest rate is mixed (ECA, 1991).

It is also untenable to insist on the drastic withdrawal of subsidies and claim to be pursuing human resource development, equity and the expansion of domestic production. In education and health, it is clear that reliance on free market pricing will penalize the poor and the weak, and thus be highly inequitable. In these cases, subsidies are not only to redistribute resources toward the poor, but also to offer them incentives to participate in modern social services, so the withdrawal of such subsidies has been causing an alarming relapse into illiteracy, falling enrolment in education and the reappearance of diseases like kwashiorkor, tuberculosis, measles and small-pox which had been wiped out in the 1960s and 1970s (Jolly et al, 1987). With a massive agricultural support programme in the USA and a Common Agricultural Policy (CAP) costing billions of dollars annually, it is double-standard for the Fund and Bank to ban such subsidies in African countries. The suggestion that the Western countries can afford subsidies but Africa cannot is simply a subterfuge because the USA is also highly indebted and each country must exercise its sovereign right over resource allocation to its national priorities.

The fine pin-pointing of adjustment measures such as a credit ceiling of 30.8 per cent or budget deficit of 3.7 per cent is similarly contested in orthodox adjustment programmes. The database for this type of sensitive parametric targeting is simply not available in Africa. Even if it were, in real life, a range in policy measures is more flexible and easier to achieve than a pin-point target whose empirical basis is often dubious. So why 3.7 per cent for budget deficit instead of 3.1 or 3.9 or 3.0 per cent? Administratively, these fine targets are difficult to achieve without under or over-shooting, and thus constitute a built-in commitment to failure in adjustment programmes.

The imposition of orthodox adjustment policies on a country-by-country basis then violates the Bank's rhetorical commitment to African integration (World Bank, LTPS, 1989). While this atomistic treatment is the source of the enormous power of the Fund and Bank over the debtor countries, and is an expression of their individualist ideology, it is inappropriate for African countries. It undermines the harmonization of policies and programmes required for the promotion of sub-regional and regional cooperation. The market catechism of orthodox adjustment programmes has a similar effect of weakening sub-regional and regional planning for collective recovery and transformation through a pragmatic blend of planning and pricing in resource allocation.

The point has been made that orthodox adjustment programmes generate de-industrialization in Africa through their emphasis on the pursuit of the comparative advantage of African countries in primary production; their advocacy of generalized export promotion; import liberalization for foreign manufacturers; informal sector industrialization; excessive devaluation that forces the closure of import-dependent industries; and the privatization of public enterprises that promote intermediate and heavy industries. Thus it is inconceivable that African countries should be guided in Fund–Bank programmes to rely on the informal sector for their industrialization. The celebration of the bloated informal sector created by orthodox adjustment programmes, as a result of its massive retrenchment and systematic undermining of formal sector activities, is also misguided.

Import liberalization has also facilitated the dumping of sub-standard foreign manufactures in Africa, undermining the prospects for local infant industries. Excessive and frequent currency devaluation under orthodox SAPs make the costs of imported raw materials, intermediate products and spare parts for local industries prohibitive, lead to factory closures and serious capacity under-utilization hovering around a 30 per cent average for Africa. Fledgling state industries in cement, iron and steel, vehicle assembly and fertilizers are attacked by the Fund and Bank as inefficient producers of goods that could be imported more cheaply – as if these industries were not built in the same ways in advanced countries. In these ways, orthodox adjustment programmes have been systematically undermining the industrialization programmes of African countries – under the thinly disguised excuse of static efficiency that is inappropriate for long-run structural transformation. It should be pointed out here that on the basis of static efficiency criteria, Britain would never have had a major textiles sub-sector because it does not produce cotton, nor would the industrialized countries have been producing rubber products, vegetable oil, uranium, copper and similar products in which they have no clear comparative advantage.

Impact of orthodox adjustment

The controversy over the impact of IMF–World Bank stabilization and SAPs has been the most publicised area of the adjustment debate. This is especially with respect to the widely publicised disagreement between two major UN institutions on the subject – the IMF–World Bank, on one hand, and the Economic Commission for Africa (ECA), on the other, over the impact of adjustment on Africa's growth in the 1980s. A joint report with the UNDP, titled *Africa's Adjustment and Growth in the 1980s* (World Bank, 1988) claimed that adjustment programmes were succeeding in African countries. The ECA disagreed in its rebuttal titled *Statistics and Policies* (ECA, 1989).

The debate on the impact of SAPs in Africa involves the following major sample sources in chronological order:

1. ECA's *African Priority Programme of Economic Recovery* (APPER) for 1986–90 which was adopted as the *UN's Programme of Action for African Economic Recovery and Development* (UN-PAAERD) for 1986–90;
2. 1987 Conferences for the evaluation of SAPs by the Scandinavian Institute of African Studies and the Institute for African Alternatives (IFAA);
3. UNICEF's 'adjustment with a human face' of 1987;
4. World Bank-UNDP report of 1989 titled *Africa's Adjustment and Growth in the 1980s and its Adjustment Lending, Ten Years of Experience*;
5. ECA's 1989 rebuttal of this report;
6. UN General Assembly's 1988 mid-term review of UN-PAAERD;
7. The *African Alternative Framework to Structural Adjustment Programmes for Socio-Economic Recovery and Transformation* (AAF-SAP) of July 1989;
8. World Bank's 1989 *Long-term Perspective Study* (LTPS);
9. 1990 evaluation of conference on SAPs in Tripoli, Libya by the African Regional Centre for Applied Research and Training in Social Development (ACARTSOD);
10. World Institute for Development Economics Research (WIDER) study titled *Varieties of Stabilisation Experience* (Oxford, 1988).
11. The World Bank's 1990 World Development Report titled *Poverty*, UNNDP's *Human Development Report* of 1990 and ILO's *Labour Review*.

These sample assessments of the impact of orthodox adjustment programmes can be classified into the following four groups:

Table 4.1 Classification of sampled impact assessment of SAPs

Support SAPs	Against or critical of SAPs	On socio-political impact of SAPs	On alternatives to SAPs
4, 8	1, 2, 3, 5, 6, 7, 8, 9, 10, 11.	2, 3, 9, 10 (SIAS-IFAA, UNICEF, ARCASOD, Poverty).	(1), 2, 3, 7, 8. (APPER/UN-PAAERD, IFAA, UNICEF, AAF-SAP, LTPS).

Note: Numbers refer to the listing of assessments above from (1) to (11).

Thus it is only the studies by the World Bank and the UNDP (*Adjustment and Growth*) and the Bank's LTPS, of 1989, which calls for "new generation SAPs", that explicitly endorse the impact of SAPs. The IMF, or course, is also supportive of SAPs along with the major sponsors of the Fund and Bank. This is why Lomé IV[1] is also based on these orthodox SAPs. *Adjustment with Growth* concluded from the evaluation of SAPs that the adjustment programmes have been successful in the "strongly adjusting" countries as in Table 4.2.

Similarly, the Bank's LTPS endorses the major impact of orthodox SAPs so far and promises "new generation SAPs" and the introduction of long-term programmes for the resumption of economic growth in African countries. But the study raises some doubts about the efficacy of SAPs in tackling the region's structural problems. The LTPS also indicates an "emerging consensus" among the parties to the adjustment debate – especially some agreement between it and the ECA on such matters as the necessity for adjustment with growth, the need for medium-term adjustment programmes, priority to human resource development for the pursuit of people-centred development and the need for increased flexibility in the design of adjustment programmes. Unfortunately, the Bank in the LTPS does not say when these areas of consensus will be translated into practical policies on these grounds.

The remaining sampled assessments of SAPs are either openly opposed to ongoing adjustment programmes, or very critical of them. Four of these critical evaluations focus on the social and political impact of SAPs, while five proffer policy alternatives to orthodox SAPs as indicated in Table 4.1. The socio-political impact evaluations are those of the Scandinavian institute of African Studies (SIAS) and the Institute for African Alternatives (IFAA), UNICEF, the African

1. Lomé IV is the Fourth Lomé Convention on trade, aid, debt and adjustment between the EEC and the African, Caribbean and Pacific countries (i.e., ACP countries).

Table 4.2 Growth of gross domestic product (GDP) in Africa, 1980–87 (%)

Country groups	1980/81	1981/82	1982/83	1983/84	1984/85	1985/86	1986/87	1980/87 Average
Strong adjusting	–3.01	0.33	–3.85	–4.31	6.33	2.82	–1.97	–0.53
Weak adjusting	5.44	3.46	0.66	–1.29	0.13	4.01	1.88	2.00
Non-adjusting	3.92	3.35	3.53	3.68	6.40	3.62	–2.51	3.50
Sub-Saharan Africa	–1.05	1.01	–2.37	–2.94	5.44	3.09	–1.48	0.24
North Africa	–2.27	3.12	3.63	2.78	1.90	0.19	1.29	1.73
Africa total	–1.52	1.81	–0.06	–0.66	3.98	1.92	–0.38	0.73

Sources: World Bank data files; ECA, *Statistics and Policies*, p. 10.

Notes: (1) These are in constant 1980 US dollars and market prices.
(2) Average annual growth rates are arithmetic averages (preliminary).

Regional Centre for Applied Research and Training in Social Development (ACARTSOD) and the 1990 Poverty report by the World Bank. The SAP assessments that present alternative programmes for recovery with transformation are those of APPER–UN–PAAERD, SIAS–IFAA Conferences, UNICEF, AAF–SAP, the World Bank's LTPS and the UNDP.

Overall, the sampled evaluations of SAPs that reject them or are very critical emphasize two common conclusions: first, that the orthodox stabilization and SAPs have been disastrous failures with few success stories – even with respect to their own performance criteria such as growth rate, inflation, balance of payments, deficit financing and exports; and, second, that the human costs or social effects of these Fund–Bank programmes have been alarming, especially on vulnerable social groups like women, children, rural-urban poor and the aged – just as their political impact has been quite negative. These are reflected in the main conclusions of each of these assessments as summarized below for the main institutions that produced the negative evaluations, namely, the Scandinavian Institute of African Studies (SIAS), IFAA, ECA, UNICEF, UN General Assembly, ILO, UNDP and the World Bank itself. The conference of SIAS in 1987, which drew participants from several African countries, North America and Europe, concluded that orthodox stabilization and SAPs were too short term to be effective, and although they were improving some financial balances, especially budget deficits, this was at the cost of lower economic performance and traumatic social effects. The report and proceedings of the IFAA conference in October 1987 in London also contained case-studies of the disastrous economic, social and political impact of Fund–Bank programmes in 19 African countries (Onimode, 1988 and 1989).

The UN's Economic Commission for Africa (ECA) has three reports on the negative impact of Fund–Bank programmes. But for some inexplicable reason, the Fund and Bank give the wrong impression that only the ECA opposes their failed adjustment programmes. In APPER, which was adopted as UN–PAAERD in a petrified version (some even maintain that UN–PAAERD resembles the discredited World Bank's *Berg Report* of 1981), the ECA raised alarm at the rapid deterioration of the African crisis that reflected the failure of Fund–Bank programmes (ECA, 1986). It then proffered alternative policies in a cooperative programme between Africa and the international community. Then in 1988 it issued its famous rebuttal to the World Bank–UNDP report, claiming that adjustment was generating growth (ECA, 1988). It presented the following table to show that this claim was based on the unacceptable manipulation of

Table 4.3 Summary of economic performance indicators, 1980–87

Indicator	Period	With strong reform programmes	With weak or no reform programme	With strong reform programmes	With weak or no reform programmes
1. Growth of GDP	1980/84	1.4	1.5	1.2	0.7
(constant 1980 prices)	1985/87	2.8	2.7	3.8	1.5
2. Agricultural production	1980/84	1.1	1.3	1.4	1.8
	1985/87	2.6	1.5	3.4	2.6
3. Growth of export volume	1980/84	−1.3	−3.1	−0.7	−5.7
	1985/87	(−11.0)	(−0.9)	(−4.7)	(−2.1)
		4.2	0.2	4.9	−3.3
		(−2.0)	(−2.5)	(3.5)	(−6.0)
4. Growth of import volume	1985/87	1.7	−2.7	6.1	−4.0
import volume (excluding		(−7.7)	(−3.0)	(7.4)	(−2.2)
oil exporters)		4.8(6.8)	–	–	–
5. Growth of real domestic	1980/84	−8.1	−3.7	−3.5	−7.0
investment	1985/87	−0.9	−7.0	1.9	−4.8
6. Gross domestic savings	1982/84	9.9	2.3	7.8	0.9
(% of GDP)	1986/87	10.7	6.0	10.7	5.6
7. Growth of per capita	1980/84	−2.3	−1.1	−2.4	−1.5
consumption (real)	1985/87	−0.4	−0.5	0.7	−0.9

Note: Averages unweighted except as noted. Figures in parentheses are weighted averages of country growth rates based on total values summed across countries.

Sources: 1. *World Bank, Africa's Adjustment and Growth in the 1980s,* March 1989.

statistics and that the objective situation showed falling growth rates in most African countries.

In addition, Table 4.4 shows the general and sectoral failures of orthodox SAPs across Africa – where per capita income and consumption levels fell by 2.6 per cent annually from 1980 to 1988 and total employment declined by 16 per cent.

Table 4.4 Decline of growth rates of Africa's economic indicators, 1978–88 (percentages)

Indicators	1978	1988
1. GDP per capita ($)	854	565
2. Growth of GDP per capita	3.03	–0.88
3. Share of investment in GDP	25.2	15.8
4. Annual rate of inflation	15.1 (1980)	21.3
5. Annual growth rate of agriculture	1.5	2.3
6. Annual growth rate of industry	7.5	4.9
7. Annual growth rate of mining	7.2	4.7
8. Annual growth rate of exports	11.2	3.8
9. Annual growth rate of imports	9.9	0.3
10. Current account or foreign trade deficit ($ billion)	3.9	20.3
11. Total external debt ($ billion)	48.3	230.0

Source: A. Adedeji (1990) *The African Alternative* (ECA: Addis Ababa).

Subsequently, in 1989, ECA produced the *African Alternative* to orthodox SAPs, (AAF–SAP) which summarized the negative economic, social and political impact of SAPs as well as their theoretical defects before offering an alternative programme for simultaneous adjustment-with-transformation (ECA, 1989).

As the adjustment debate gathered momentum in 1987, UNICEF launched its *Adjustment with a Human Face* (R. Jolly et al., 1987). It argued strongly that orthodox Fund–Bank programmes were imposing severe hardships and traumatic suffering on the vulnerable social groups, and called for a more humane approach to recovery. This report is the basis of the introduction of the Social Dimension of Adjustment (SDA) programme by the World Bank, which was first experimented on Ghana as the Programme of Action for the Mitigation of the Social Cost of Adjustment (PAMSCAD). But one problem with UNICEF's "Adjustment with a human face" is the fact that it is disturbingly silent on what should be the fate of the on-going SAPs that generate the horrendous social costs. As long as these SAPs remain in place, the human suffering will persist.

Similarly, the UN General Assembly's mid-term review of UN-PAAERD in 1988 revealed some chilling statistics about the negative economic and social impact of orthodox SAPs. These include the death of over 1,000 children per day in Africa, pervasive starvation and malnutrition that have led to the revival of several diseases that had previously been wiped out, rising mortality rates, falling educational enrolment and the continued general decline of African economies. It also revealed that the international community had done little towards its planned contribution of about $42 billion toward Africa's recovery as proposed in UN-PAAERD.

The ILO has supplemented these assessments of on-going SAPs with in-depth empirical studies across Africa that are reported in its *Labour Review* (ILO, several years). They confirm that real wages and incomes have fallen by about 50 per cent since 1980, that unemployment at all levels has risen massively and that living standards have been declining precipitously (see especially ILO, 1989). These have been the collective consequences of massive retrenchment, deregulation, drastic budget and credit squeeze, rising interest rates, massive devaluation and sharply increased import costs and the privatization of public enterprises and resulting job losses.

In their defence, the IMF, World Bank and their supporters insist that adjustment is a necessity, no matter how painful. They claim that adjustment is succeeding in raising exports, reducing budget deficits, inflation and balance of payments deficits, producing better pricing and more efficient resource allocation. They even maintain that adjustment has been generating economic growth and success stories in Ghana, Mauritius and Cote d'Ivoire – before this last "success" collapsed, especially when the country doubled cocoa exports and its export revenue fell by 50 per cent during 1988–89. In its *1991 World Development Report,* the World Bank stated that SAPs increased growth in Nigeria, Ghana, Togo, Kenya and Tunisia but that there was deterioration in Cameroon, Liberia, Sudan and Zaire.

The Bretton Woods institutions also claim that the failure of orthodox adjustment programmes is due mainly to their poor implementation in the adjusting countries. They also maintain that the appropriate method for programme evaluation should not be the usual comparative static approach of assessing the situation before and after the adoption of the programmes. Rather, they claim, the post-programme situation should be compared with what it would have been without their adjustment programmes. But this is clearly an untenable method because it panders to metaphysics and subverts the standard approach of comparative statics in economic theory. Nobody, including the Fund and Bank, can tell what any situation would have been without a given programme because of several possible intervening factors. Thus in the African countries, without orthodox adjustment programmes, factors such as the absence of drought, more favourable commodity trade or better external debt would have greatly improved their socio-economic situation and performance. But, perhaps, the most devastating evidence against this defence of orthodox adjustment and the alleged success of on-going SAPs are the two publications of the World Bank itself and the UNDP in 1990 titled *Poverty* and *Human Development Report* respectively. After reviewing the dismal performance of the African economy since the 1980s, the Bank's *Poverty* Report concluded that Africa will be the only region in the world where per capita income will be falling right up to the 21st century (World Bank, 1990). If Fund–Bank programmes have been succeeding as claimed, this nightmare scenario should have been ruled out. Some other alarming statistics of the study are summarized below.

The UNDP's *Human Development Report* comes to similar conclusions:

> The economic crisis of the 1980s has in many countries stalled – or even reversed – earlier progress in human development . . . The economies of most developing countries slowed down in the 1980s, except in Asia, [where] they experienced a nearly continuous economic decline, and despite vigorous adjustment efforts, they were still showing sever imbalances at the end of the 1980s . . . . In Africa, income per person declined more that 25% for the region as a whole (30% taking into account the deterioration in the terms of trade). GDP did grow faster in 1985/87 than during 1980/84, but that growth was still slower than the growth in population, and incomes per person fell at roughly the same rate in countries with strong reform programmes as in countries with weak or no reform programmes. Investment fell more than 9% a year, and per capita consumption 1% to 2% a year . . . . Poverty is growing fastest in Africa, with the number of absolute poor having increased by about two-thirds between 1970 and 1985. (UNDP, 1990; back cover and pp. 22 and 34).

Political impact of orthodox adjustment programmes

One critical impact of orthodox stabilization and SAPs omitted by most of the above assessments which deal with economic and social effects is the political effect. In a region where politics has been identified as a major factor in persistent underdevelopment and crisis, this is a significant question. The two basic issues here are the effects of these adjustment programmes on the fledgling democratization process in the region and on the fragile national sovereignty of these countries.

The effects on democratic experiments centre around the negotiations of these programmes, their implementation procedure, dissent management and response mechanisms. Thus it is disturbing that the negotiations of these Fund–Bank programmes are rarely ever subjected to broad national discussion or debate. Rather, the negotiations tend to be conducted almost secretly or clandestinely between officials of the IMF and World Bank, on one hand, and a few top executives (President, Ministers of Finance, Planning and Trade, and selected top bureaucrats) of the adjusting countries, on the other. In some countries, major reform policies such as devaluation, import liberalization, de-regulation and the raising of interest rates, mass retrenchment and privatization are negotiated with this handful of top officials. Indeed, the more unpopular the policy measures or adjustment programmes, the more clandestine their negotiations tend to be. And yet these are policies and programmes with far-reaching effects on entire populations that should be widely debated in national assemblies, mass media and other fora.

Perhaps worse than the negotiation process is the bureaucratic implementation of these Fund–Bank programmes. Avoiding political processes with mass mobilization and popular participation of broad social forces, the high-handed and elitist implementation of orthodox adjustment programmes has a built-in commitment to failure. The secretive negotiations and bureaucratic implementation of these programmes make them extremely unpopular. Hence the need for authoritarian regimes and neo-fascist coups for their adoption and execution. Orthodox stabilization and adjustment programmes encourage the pervasive undermining of democracy and the militarization of politics across Africa. There is hardly any SAP that has ever passed the test of an open electoral process.

For these reasons, Fund–Bank programmes operate to undermine both political and financial accountability in African countries. As expected, since there is no democratic participation in the negotiation and implementation of these programmes, there can be no accountability. This aggravates the problem of pervasive lack of democracy and accountability in Africa in two ways. First, national governments and officials feel encouraged to pass the buck of accountability for these programmes to the IMF and World Bank. This is particularly seductive, as the officials of these Bretton Woods institutions are highly visible as supervisors in sensitive institutions like Central Banks and the Ministries of Finance, Planning, Foreign Trade and Industries. In the circumstances, however, even when national governments agree with popular demand for the replacement or modification of some of the adjustment programmes, they are often overruled by their Washington overlords. Where some uninformed African governments naively present these authoritarian SAPs as their own national programmes, they resist financial and political accountability for them by appealing to the rhetoric of the inevitability of these failed programmes.

Repressive dissent management is then employed as a second mechanism for the denial of accountability in the adjusting countries. The fascist repression often includes forcible military intervention to break adjustment stalemates, brutal killings by the police (and the military in some countries) during "IMF riots" as in Nigeria, Zambia, Morocco, Cote d'Ivoire, etc., and the incarceration of opponents of these repressive austerity measures. The brutality of the state in the containment of these SAP riots then tends to reinforce the unstructured violence of the anti-SAP demonstrations. In the process, Fund–Bank SAPs have become an additional institutional source of pervasive strife and political instability against the tenuous legitimacy of the post-colonial state in Africa. The initial largely economic crisis in the region has thus been expanding dangerously into pervasive socio-political instability and disintegration.

The second major political impact of IMF and World Bank stabilization and adjustment programmes in Africa is the systematic undermining of the sovereignty of the post-colonial state in Africa. There are several alarming aspects of this phenomenon. One is the atomization of the state which is the political analogy of the informalization of the economy. The African state, like its counterpart in the rest of the Third World, has been reduced to a mere "*adjustment state*" – to adjust the national economy and population to the rapacious requirements of the creditor countries, for the repayment of immoral external debts, the dumping of manufactured food imports, repatriation of profits for multinational corporations (MNCs) and unhindered penetration and domination by foreign capital.

The foreign design and imposition of these Fund–Bank stabilization and adjustment programmes is another feature. Adjustment has become a convenient excuse for an offensive to systematically weaken and undermine the state in Africa and the rest of the Third World. Under the excuse that public enterprises have failed and the search for a solution to the fiscal crisis of the state, orthodox adjustment is frenetically rolling back the state and the public sector across Africa. Though this is thinly disguised as a programme for raising overall economic efficiency, it is evident that it is a critical element in the task assigned to the Fund and Bank to construct and maintain an international capitalist system in which private capital and goods can move freely across countries without any control or hindrance from national governments. The Bretton Woods institutions do not allow the adjusting countries to design their own reform programmes which the Fund and Bank can then assist and improve. Rather, there is a paternalistic take-it-or-leave-it posture. Even when some adjusting countries do not need SAPs, they are required by the Fund and Bank to adopt them; and when these countries design national recovery programmes, the Bretton Woods institutions quickly set them aside and substitute their own Policy Framework Paper (PFP) for orthodox programmes. Yet, they hypocritically claim that their role in the adjustment process is merely to support national initiatives.

The Fund and the Bank have rapidly become new colonial supervisors of the adjusting countries. In this paternalistic role, they post their staff to sensitive institutions in African countries to ensure adequate foreign exchange allocation for external debt service at unbearable ratios of over 40 per cent of annual export earnings, to supervise national budgets, bank credit allocations and tariff policy. National budgets, foreign exchange allocation, expenditure proposals, revision of tariff regulations and rates, exchange and interest rates have to be approved or endorsed by the Fund or Bank *before* they can be implemented. In some cases, revised national tariff measures have been rejected by the World Bank as in Nigeria in 1988 – largely because the Bank prefers low uniform tariff rates, which favour import-dumping but offer little protection to domestic production activities, especially infant industries and food production.

At the international level, the political impact of orthodox adjustment programmes has made African and other Third World countries pathetically docile and increasingly marginalized. A major index of this is the low priority that has been accorded to the demand for a New International Economic Order (NIEO) from the early 1980s. Indeed, the World Bank has pointedly proposed a substitute for the NIEO for African countries – the creation of a *Global Coalition for Africa* (World Bank, *LTPS,* 1989, p. 193). As the debtor countries have had their diplomatic energies tied down to begging for foreign debt relief and SAP negotiations they have tended to become relatively docile in the international arena, much to the advantage of the creditor countries. This is how even the negotiations of the settlement of Africa's major regional conflicts in Angola, Mozambique, Liberia, Sudan, Ethiopia and South Africa have become almost the exclusive prerogatives of Western capitals and Moscow.

In such ways, the political impact of Fund–Bank stabilization and adjustment programmes has been a systematic weakening and essential marginalization of the state in Africa, through a direct affront on its traditional sovereignty and the reversal of the gains of democratization since flag independence.

Adjustment or delinking debate

Another important aspect of the adjustment debate has been termed "adjustment or delinking". Here adjustment is really readjustment, because Africa and the rest of the Third World, as the periphery of world capitalism, have been adjusting continuously to the reproductive requirements of the metropolitan centre of world capitalism. This adjustment typically becomes tough and traumatic during the downturn (crisis, depression or recession) phase of world capitalist expansion. In boom periods, this adjustment is easier as export prices are high, capital is available, employment expands, etc. Adjustment thus becomes a question of grafting internal balances and growth (not development as such) on to the concessions and possibilities granted by the world capitalist system. Adjustment to world capitalism thus maintains and reproduces unequal and polarized development. Though this adjustment does not overtly imply the absolute negation of growth:

> Growth through adjustment is in fact an *ideological* justification of a growth realized in favour of a minority that imposes its development, to make its class domination permanent. This growth through adjustment is perverse in the precise sense of unequal growth, reproducing and deepening the heterogeneity and sectoral and societal disparities while rendering the external positions even more fragile, that is, making the drawbacks of adjustment even more evident. Through growth and adjustment, the shaping of the societies of the periphery by external constraints is reproduced in new forms. (Mahjoub, 1990, p.167).

The periphery of world capitalism has thus always been engaged in never-ending adjustment to the demands and constraints of the dominant capital. "The centres are 'restructured', the peripheries are 'adjusted' to these restructurings. Never the reverse", stated Mahjoub.

Delinking, therefore, is refusal to submit to the unbearable demands of world capitalism and rejection of the alleged rationality or optimality of the system of world prices. It involves the gradual establishment of new societies that makes popular nation-building possible. As the logical product of unequal development, delinking creates a new social space that is open for popular participation with greater equality in the relations of distribution. It leads to the acquisition of spaces of relative autonomy in relation to the world capitalist system.

This adjustment–delinking debate thus revives the debate over the "non-capitalist path" of development. It thus constitutes a sharp ideological rendition of the adjustment debate. Delinking, rather than adjustment, should be pursued, to achieve the rapid transformation of African economies. There is a clear link between the *adjustment-transformation* debate and the *adjustment-delinking* controversy. The former accepts adjustment but states that it is inadequate, the latter rejects adjustment as perverse and demands de-linking – some have called this "*selective closure*" in a more conservative context. But both the transformation and delinking variants accept the need for rapid development and transformation. The main difference is modality – transformers suggest that structural transformation is possible with the re-orientation of adjustment but supporters of delinking deny this. Their essential unity is the need to transcend adjustment in order to launch Africa's transformation.

The end of adjustment debate

Like "the end of ideology" rhetoric (Lowi, 1969) the end of the adjustment debate has a double but interrelated implication. One is that the debate has served its theoretical and practical utility. The second implication of the end of adjustment debate is its termination. Clearly this will be quite protracted, both because while the adjustment process is continuing, so will its discussion and debate, and because even after the current adjustment process has ended (though adjustment itself is a continuous process in all economies), students of history and posterity will have the final word in debating it.

But for our limited purpose here, the utility of the adjustment debate is no longer in serious doubt, while its termination in the direction of speeding-up and improving the adjustment process itself is increasingly sought. On the utility of the adjustment debate, there is little doubt that it has clarified the six major aspects of the controversy, namely, conceptualization, sponsorship, conditionalities, policies, economic impact and socio-political effects. The debate has greatly sharpened understanding on these issues through the vast literature and empirical evidence that it has generated.

The level of consensus on these issues, may be summarized in Table 4.5.

Table 4.5 The state of debate on adjustment

Almost full agreement	Partial agreement	Major disagreement
(1) Conceptualization of adjustment	Adjustment policies	Sponsorship of adjustment
(2) Adverse social and political impact	Economic impact	Conditionalities

Thus most parties to the adjustment debate now accept that adjustment or stabilization alone is inadequate and that it should be pursued simultaneously with economic growth and structural transformation. This has always been the position of African countries and the World Bank now endorses it in terms of its new concern with global poverty and its *African Capacity Building Initiative* (ACBI) with the UNDP and the African Development Bank (ADB), while the UNDP sees this need also with respect to human development in the design of its Human Development Index (HDI). It remains, however, to link these initiatives with the urgent replacement of on-going SAPs in order to put explicit adjustment-with-transformation programmes in place along the lines of the *African Alternative* to SAP – rather than grafting piecemeal programmes like the Social Dimension of Adjustment (SDA), ACDBI and HDI onto the failed and inappropriate on-going SAPs. Similarly, the realization of the catastrophic social impact of orthodox adjustment is what prompted the SDA. But here again, it is more urgent to terminate the current SAPs that generate the social trauma than to maintain the futile effort of trying to contain their negative social effects. And more attention also must be directed to the arrest of the adverse political impact of on-going adjustment programmes. More rhetoric from the West in support of democratic ideals is insufficient.

On the adjustment policies and their economic impact, however, the adjustment debate has only produced partial agreement. Some of the current adjustment policies are now acknowledged to be inappropriate and in need of modification or replacement. Thus massive, generalized and persistent devaluation has been generating excessive inflation without restoring balance of payments equilibrium. Similarly, high interest rates, retrenchment without redeployment, drastic budget and credit squeeze across-the-board and doctrinaire privatization are now realized to be inappropriate and should be avoided. But there is still strong disagreement on other policies like free market pricing, primacy of exchange rate policy, subsidy withdrawal and generalized liberalization. Moreover, even the partial agreement on some of the policies is yet to be translated into consistent alternative policies on the ground.

The negative economic impact of current SAPs is also partially agreed upon, as indicated by the Bank in the LTPS and its report on *Poverty* as well as the UNDP's report on human development. But there is still controversy on the sectors and activities in which these SAPs have failed and the appropriate remedies for the adverse economic effects. Thus in its proposed "new generation SAPs", the World Bank is silent on the fate of on-going SAPs and the alternative policies that it would support for reviving critical activities like agriculture, industry, technology and overall structural transformation. Its "strategic agenda for the 1990s" for sub-Saharan Africa (World Bank, LTPS, 1987; Ch.9) is silent on these crucial questions, while its agreement on the primacy of African cooperation and integration stops only at market integration without the equally important issue of production integration.

The emerging consensus in the adjustment debate also does not extend to the sponsorship of adjustment programmes or to conditionalities. By launching its long-term perspective study (LTPS), the Bank and Fund give the impression that the sponsorship and design of adjustment programmes will continue as before. This is despite the lengthy rhetoric in the LTPS that the Bretton Woods institutions are only acting in a supportive role to the African countries. Yet they will not allow African countries to initiate and formulate their national adjustment-with-transformation programmes to which the multilateral financial institutions can react by assisting and modifying them.

The Fund, Bank and creditor countries seem even less willing to yield ground on their harsh conditionalities. Rather, they have extended them to other North-South programmes – such as the Lomé Convention, which was not subject to conditionality until December 1989 during the start of Lomé IV, to borrowing from ODA, drawing from ESAF, the International Commodity Fund and even from bilateral facilities. Hence the impression that these harsh conditionalities are being imposed on African countries to ensure their effective domination and exploitation under a new colonialism.

It is also for these reasons that African countries demand an end to the adjustment debate and the urgent resumption of their development. After losing the decade of the 1980s, there is widespread consensus that the 1990s must see the relaunching of the region's interrupted development process alongside its accelerated recovery. This requires the urgent implementation of the policies implied by the areas of emerging agreement in the adjustment debate so far. African countries have, therefore, to take the necessary policy actions in order to initiate their accelerated recovery-with-transformation and call on the Bretton Woods institutions and the rest of the international community to support the process.

Chapter 5

The African alternative to orthodox SAPs

Background and necessity for the African alternative

> The overall assessment of orthodox adjustment programmes has led to the conclusion that, although these programmes aim at restoring growth, generally through the achievement of fiscal and external balances and the free play of market forces, these objectives cannot be achieved without addressing the fundamental structural bottlenecks of African economies. Consequently, at the beginning of 1988, the ECA with the financial support of UNDP embarked on a search for an African alternative framework to structural adjustment programmes that would address simultaneously both adjustment and structural transformation problems of the African economies. This exercise received great encouragement from the General Assembly of the United Nations when, during the mid-term review of UN–PAAERD at its forty-third session, it called upon African countries to increase their efforts in the search for a viable conceptual and practical framework for economic structural adjustment programmes in keeping with the long-term development objectives and strategies at the national, sub-regional and regional levels. (ECA, *African Alternative Framework to Structural Adjustment Programmes for Socio-Economic Recovery and Transformation, AAF-SAP.*

The *African Alternative Framework* to orthodox SAPs (AAF-SAP) is a product of history, controversy and necessity. Historically, it is the culmination of a process that can be traced back to the early 1980s, when African countries started the process of systematic and coherent intellectual response to the region's crisis of underdevelopment. With the production of the *Lagos Plan of Action, LPA* (OAU, 1981) for Africa's development from 1980 to year 2000 as the first major collective blueprint for the region, the need for a short-to-medium-term version of the LPA was created.

The politics of adjustment later provided additional impetus for this search for a regional medium-term development programme. This need became increasingly obvious after the 1983 publication of the ECA's *Long-term Perspective* of the African economy (ECA, 1983). But the adjustment debate itself threw two challenges for the preparation of the *African Alternative Framework* that would deal concretely with the region's structural bottlenecks. One was the frequent insistence of the Bretton Woods institutions and their supporters that critics of their orthodox adjustment programmes should realise that there was no alternative or that they should provide an alternative to their unpopular SAPs. Indeed, as late as mid-1989, the military government in Nigeria bullied the critics of SAP by declaring that there was no alternative. Needless to say, the critics countered with suggestions of several alternatives, one of which was contained in the report of the 1987 conference of the Institute for African Alternatives (IFAA), (IFAA, 1988). SAP critics also rebutted the government's no-alternative-to-SAP by offering several formulations, including a National Reconstruction Programme (*Newswatch,* June-September, 1989). These challenges prompted the preparation of the *African Alternative Framework.* As indicated by the quotation at the beginning of this chapter, the mid-term review of UN-PAAERD in 1988 also threw another challenge to African countries to search for a regional framework for dealing with their recovery and development problems. The ECA took these challenges seriously and immediately started the preparation of the African Alternative Framework.

Besides these historical and controversial catalysts, the preparation of the African Alternative was also motivated by objective necessity: the requirement to cope with accumulating empirical evidence on the failure of Fund–Bank stabilization and adjustment programmes, the rapid deterioration of the African crisis since the launching of APPER and UN–PAAERD in 1986, and the increasing realization of the need for a conceptual framework for pursuing Africa's adjustment and long-term development objectives as articulated in the Lagos Plan of Action. Thus according to the Report of the UN Secretary-General on the mid term review of UN–PAAERD the annual growth rate of GDP for Africa as a whole fell from 1.0 per cent in 1986 to 0.8 per cent by 1987, due largely to the poor performance of the export sector. Consequently, the growth of GDP per capita also declined by 2 per cent in 1986 and 2.2 per cent in 1987. In about 28 of the 50 member states of the ECA, the growth of GDP in 1986 and 1987 was either negative or less than the population growth rate. Food production was most seriously affected, and the regional food deficit increased with food-aid requirements rising by more than 45 per cent during 1987–88 for the 45 countries of developing sub-Saharan Africa. Most African countries were thus experiencing economic decline and serious social distress (Adedeji, 1990, Ch. 4).

The sharp controversy between the World Bank and ECA on the economic performance of Africa by 1988 underscored these concerns. From the point of view of Africa, that controversy represented a growing loss of confidence in the efficacy of orthodox adjustment programmes. This dictated an urgent need to articulate an alternative programme for the accelerated recovery and transformation of the region. If there was to be any possibility of reversing the region's steep decline, the theoretical and empirical questioning of on-going orthodox adjustment programmes had to be backed up intellectually with the development of a collective and alternative regional programme.

Conceptualization of the African alternative

The African Alternative Framework to Structural Adjustment Programmes for Socio-Economic Recovery and Transformation (AAF–SAP) is a holistic approach and *not* a ready programme to be applied indiscriminately to all countries. It provides a conceptual basis for the appropriate design of national programmes – which will differ from country to country – for the pursuit of accelerated adjustment-with-transformation. The two interrelated parts of the framework are:

- the conceptual or theoretical framework for the design, implementation and monitoring of alternative adjustment programmes in each African country; and
- alternative policy directions or strategies, policy instruments and specific measures to be applied for the realization of the objectives of the adjustment and development process.

The essence of offering an alternative for the pursuit of Africa's recovery and development therefore starts at the conceptual level. The African Alternative Framework does this in four central areas:

African context

Understanding of the concrete context of adjustment and transformation is crucial. This requires a clear comprehension of the problematic political economy of Africa and its major structural bottlenecks. The long failure of this understanding is the original defect in orthodox Fund–Bank stabilization and adjustment programmes. This objective reality or African context is what provides the norm of adjustment, its relevant objectives, adjustment paradigm and the sequencing of the processes of recovery and development;

Philosophy and paradigm

Though these are not stated explicitly in AAF–SAP, the framework is informed by the philosophy of African Humanism and its paradigm flows from this as people-centred development. These contrast with the empiricist philosophy underlying the ideology of laissez-faire or liberal capitalism and anti-statism of orthodox adjustment programmes, whose neoclassical paradigm focuses on "things" or commodities, the search for equilibrium or balances, gradualism, individualism and free market pricing. Though the African Alternative does not articulate an explicit ideology, a careful reading of it shows that it is informed by the ideology of mixed economy and democratic populism. These contrast also with the Social Market Economy of the Scandinavian countries which the World Bank recommends to African countries (Maastritch Conference, 1990, and LTPS, p. 187). These strive to put people and their critical needs and welfare on centre stage in the adjustment and transformation process of the African Alternative Framework. The UNDP's Human Development Index (HDI) of 1990 also derives from this people-centred development;

Sequencing of adjustment and transformation

Both adjustment and transformation or development are to be pursued simultaneously or concurrently in the African Alternative Framework, rather than as sequential processes as accorded by orthodox SAPs. With the lost decade of the 1980s, Africa can no longer afford to put its development or structural transformation on hold and pursue elusive stabilization or adjustment of financial balances as prescribed by orthodox adjustment;

Objectives of adjustment process

AAF–SAP defines the objectives of the adjustment process as the pursuit of the long-term development objectives of African economies as stipulated in the LPA (see Chapter 2). The basic idea here is the logic that even the longest run is a series of short and medium terms, and this rejects the Keynesian myopia that "in the long-run, we are all dead". As adjustment and transformation are to be pursued concurrently, the process of adjustment should also advance the achievement of long-term development objectives. In this way, adjustment will transcend its orthodox fire-fighting conception and simultaneously address the more durable structural bottlenecks of the economy.

From all these, it is important to emphasize the centrality of the African historical context. Unless this is analysed sympathetically and grasped firmly, no recovery programme can succeed. The substitution of alien social reality such as Keynesian inadequate demand, derived from the economies of the advanced capitalist countries, for the African context is thus, a logical "fallacy of misplaced concreteness". Any systematic and serious analysis of the political economy of African countries will reveal their deep-seated disarticulation or distorted structural linkages, lop-sided development, excessive external dependence, undue reliance on exchange activities, lack of democracy and social tensions. The fundamental root causes of these salient features of the African political economy derive from their perverse structures of production, consumption, distribution or inequality, incomes and power. These are the factors that force African countries to consume mostly what they do not produce, and to produce much of what they do not consume. And such problems will not be solved by merely pursuing financial balances.

For these reasons, the uncritical application of the competitive optimality model of orthodox SAPs to African countries is at best dubious, and often quite useless as an epistemological barrier to the understanding of the real functioning of African economies. Thus rather than perfect competition and free factor mobility, we encounter pervasive imperfect competition with monopolies and oligopolies, e.g., the multinational corporations (MNCs) that dominate mining, oil, banking, insurance, manufacturing and construction. The well-known structural rigidities, uncertainties and imperfect information in Africa also severely restrict the responsiveness of economic agents to price signals. When major export commodities take six to eight years to produce, this clearly limits the effectiveness of short-run price signals and incentives. The low levels of technology, productive capacity and productivity also mean that Africa's major problems centre round supply shortages and supply creation, rather than the orthodox adjustment pre-occupation with the manipulation of demand. It is also inappropriate to expose the majority of African producers who are peasant small-holders in isolated villages to compete in free market pricing with the giant foreign multinational monopolies that purchase their produce. The dominance of foreign capital in critical sectors of African economies also means that unbridled free competition and full liberalization will exacerbate the external dependence and exploitative de-capitalization of these countries.

It is because of the significant peculiarities of the African context that both the orientation and major policies of orthodox adjustment programmes in Africa are flawed. The glaring examples of these inappropriate strategies and policies include the sequence of stabilization or adjustment before transformation, reliance on free market forces and prices for resource allocation, full liberalization and uncritical de-regulation, withdrawal of the state from the economy, massive devaluation, drastic subsidy withdrawal across the board and severe budget and credit squeeze. These policies encounter important rigidities and even social resistance that pervert them into causing disruptions and social misery so that they are unable to raise the level of economic performance in a significant way. Hence the protracted decline and stagnation wrought on African economies by these misguided policies which are inappropriate for the African development context.

Alternative policy directions

For the pursuit of the conceptualization of recovery-with-transformation, the African Alternative Framework (AAF–SAP) identifies some basic strategies and alternative policy directions (ECA 1989). This is in clear recognition of the dead-ends to which many past and current strategies have led African economies. Examples of such empirically flawed strategies are export-led growth, import substitution industrialization (ISI), generalized export promotion, pursuit of comparative advantage in primary production, full economic liberalization and the primacy of financial stabilization.

Alternative strategies

The alternative strategies of AAF–SAP are fivefold, namely:

- vigorous pursuit of human-centred and self-sustaining development;
- priority to production activities for the transformation of Africa from an exchange economy into a production economy;
- democratization of the development process through popular participation and accountability in public affairs;
- vigorous mobilization of domestic resources and the revamping of institutions; and
- energetic pursuit of regional cooperation and integration.

Sustainable development is the central focus of full development and utilization of human resources. This is critical in a region that has experienced bursts of growth with little development, and where massive unemployment and underemployment coexist with shortages of skilled labour in strategic sectors of the economy. The transformation from an exchange economy dominated by commercial or distributive activities to a production economy requiring local production of basic needs is therefore central. The termination of prostrate external dependence and the basic contradiction between production and consumption are involved as well as the urgent increase in the productive capacity of African countries. This transformation into full production is also the surest way of utilizing human resources and providing opportunities for technological development. These require the vigorous mobilization of the region's internal resources and their effective allocation to productive use. They also need the urgent revamping and strengthening of institutions at all levels – bureaucracies, educational and health institutions, research and development centres, parastatals and private enterprises.

But AAF–SAP also underscores the basic fact that these have to be pursued not only at the national level, but also at sub-regional and regional levels. The illusion of the possibility of independent national development must be jettisoned urgently. There are very few African countries – two or three at most – that can be economically viable on their own steam. Hence effective sub-regional and regional cooperation through both market and production integration is a crucial imperative as stated in the Lagos Plan of Action (LPA). The tragedy of the non–implementation of the LPA must be redressed for the accelerated internalization of the engine of development in Africa.

The African Alternative Framework avoids the rabid economism of orthodox SAPs by emphasizing the strategic roles of non–economic factors in the recovery-with-transformation process. These are people, democracy and accountability. So AAF–SAP elaborates the necessity for the full democratization of African societies through the empowerment of the people, popular participation and binding financial and political accountability of policy-makers and other public functionaries. This is critical to the liquidation of the pervasive venality that has swindled poor African countries of billions of dollars in flight capital into fat secret foreign bank accounts in Switzerland and elsewhere.

Alternative policy directions

The successful application of these strategies for the achievement of Africa's long-term development objectives requires the pursuit of alternative policy directions. These are to ensure that the adjustment process conforms with the requirements of accelerated structural transformation in various sectors of the economy. Hence the proposed policy directions emphasize the need for overall production and export diversification, better incentives for domestic agricultural production, more efficient financial management, effective financial accountability, improved control of inflation and better external debt management. These show that financial stabilization or the restoration of monetary, fiscal and trade balances is an abiding commitment in AAF–SAP. But these financial balances must be pursued simultaneously with the urgent transformation of the basic structures of the economy and society.

The proposed alternative policy directions in the African Alternative Framework are:

- strengthening and diversification of production activities and exports, especially in agriculture and industry, for the satisfaction of the critical needs of society;
- basic realignment of the patterns of consumption with the profile of production;
- drastic reduction of prostrate import dependence and overall extroversion;
- shifting of resources from non-productive to productive activities and priority social services;
- creation of an enabling environment for accelerated recovery and sustainable development in both economic and non-economic spheres;
- increased productivity and efficient resource allocation;
- effective mobilization and utilization of resources, including elimination of waste as well as internal and external leakages;
- strengthening of human resource development, their improved utilization and the strengthening of technological capacity;
- establishment of a pragmatic balance between public and private sectors;
- improvement of the distribution of income, wealth and power among social classes, social groups and households;
- efficient management of external debt and debt servicing; and
- promotion of effective popular participation in the recovery-with-development process through full democratization, economic empowerment of the people and binding accountability, both financial and political.

The strengthening and diversification of the productive base of African economies must strike at the root of low productive capacity, excessive dependence on imports for basic national requirements, the achievement of regional food self-sufficiency, export diversification from traditional export of raw materials to the processing of these primary products and the arrest of de-industrialization. The goal here is the transformation of African economies from excessive concentration on exchange activities to focus on production activities. This requires domestic production with sub-regional and regional cooperation in production – in addition to the integration of trade. This strong focus on production is based on the realization that unless Africa develops its internal factor inputs and internalizes the productive engine of development, it will be unable to transform and sustain its economy. Moreover, just as domestic food production is strategic to the achievement of food self-sufficiency, industrial production is also the dominant and most reliable basis of national and regional power.

All these require the termination of the central contradiction of African economies – their consumption of mostly what they do not produce, and their production of mostly what they do not consume. This paradox means that the fundamental dynamics of African economies lie outside the region. It is the most graphic expression of the basic loss of autonomy in Africa, and must be redressed urgently. Without any orientation to autarchy, the region must realign its production and consumption activities through deliberate changes in imported and inappropriate consumption habits. Self-reliance must begin with a reliance on national resources and domestic production for meeting most of the basic requirements of African countries – partly to reduce the excessive demand for foreign exchange needed to import essential goods and services. In these ways, the current excessive dependence on imports can be reduced drastically.

The strengthening and diversification of the productive base and reduction of external dependence also require the increase of the currently low level of productivity, resource shift from non-productive to productive use, the elimination of waste and the plugging of various leakages. The full mobilization and efficient allocation of domestic resources as well as the development of human resources, science and technology are also involved. Raising productivity requires improved work ethos and habits through the promotion and equitable reward for the dignity of labour, improved education, training and health of the labour force as well as better techniques of production. Reduced spending on prestige and white elephant projects like huge stadia or luxury conference centres and the elimination of numerous wastes and resource leakages, into non-essential imports, flight capital and unused capacities, will also release large amounts of resources and domestic production. The full mobilization of resources requires systematic campaign against, and effective taxation of, ostentatious consumption, sustained savings campaign, rural banking to tap frittered potential savings, especially in rural areas, and more efficient utilization of resources to generate positive returns. The development of human resources, science and technology are then essential to building domestic capabilities for strengthening the productive base and for the realization of human-centred development.

A climate of incentives and supportive activities must also be created to facilitate recovery and transformation. This enabling environment includes the elimination of internal conflicts in Africa, the creation of a better and more reliable investment climate, provision of incentives and better pricing for agriculture, rehabilitation and provision of adequate infrastructures for economic and social activities as well as the effective democratization of African societies with full respect for human rights. Another important aspect of this enabling environment is the provision of *basic security* for both life and property, especially in urban areas – without this fundamental security, economic activities will be severely jeopardized. Effective popular participation with equitable reward is also important, particularly regarding the equitable participation of women in the process of recovery-with-transformation. On the basis of simple arithmetic, it should be clear that if women, who constitute about 50 per cent of the population, do not participate equitably in development, it will be difficult to achieve and sustain the transformation process. This implication applies to the need for more equitable distribution of income, resources, opportunities and power among all strata of Africa's population. Both democratization and equitable distribution are also essential to the elimination of pervasive conflicts and strife which undermine recovery and development. The achievement of a flexible and pragmatic balance between the public and private sectors is equally essential for democratic participation and for the full mobilization of development potentials.

In addition, improved external debt management is required for eliminating or relaxing the most stringent constraint on Africa's recovery and development. The total size of the external debt of each country must be objectively and firmly known, the bunching of its maturity structure should be spread out, the requirements of short, medium and long-term debt must be reconciled, the external debt service ratio should be reduced to at most 10 per cent as demanded in *Africa's Common Position on External Debt.* The *political* nature of the foreign debt crisis must be grasped to facilitate the collective organization of African countries for the cancellation of these unethical debts though the implementation of their Common Position.

Policy measures for AAF–SAP

The practical implementation of the alternative policy directions of AAF–SAP requires the elaboration and application of alternative policy packages. But it should be stressed that the policy instruments or measures proposed in the African Alternative Framework are a menu from which each country can choose according to its national circumstances and requirements. These policy measures are unlike the conditionalities and policies of IMF–World Bank orthodox stabilization and adjustment programmes that must be applied uniformly to all countries. This is unscientific and perverse as the specific policy measures required in each country have to be determined by the country itself after a detailed empirical study of the nature of its own crisis, the track record of each policy and its likely impact. The fear that countries may fail to apply some necessary policies because they are tough or politically unpopular can be resolved through dialogue between the country and the Fund–Bank and ECA.

Hence AAF-SAP policy instruments focus on three broad dimensions of the adjustment and transformation process, each of which embraces several alternative policy directions discussed above. These are:

Production

Strengthening and diversification with the generation of appropriate domestic capacities for these.

Incomes

Generation and distribution of factor incomes or patterns of reward for contributions to development – this is both aggregative and inter-personal or group-oriented. The functional distribution of income among wages, profit, interest and rent or factor rental are the sources of personal incomes.

Expenditures

Changing the patterns of government spending for the satisfaction of basic needs for individuals and among social groups. The holistic framework of the African Alternative Framework demands the integrated treatment of these critical areas. So specific policy measures have been proposed in the programme for dealing with each of these (ECA, AAF–SAP, 1989, Ch. 5).

SAP measures to be modified in AAF–SAP

The first set of issues tackled by AAF–SAP are the inappropriate orthodox adjustment policies targeted for modification under the African Alternative Framework. These are:

- Drastic budgetary cuts, which affect expenditure and subsidies on education, health and other social services and drugs. These cuts undermine human conditions, encourage massive retrenchment and jeopardize future development potential;
- Indiscriminate, generalized promotion of traditional exports of primary products alleged to maximize so-called comparative advantage – especially the promotion of such raw material exports through price incentives to "tradeables". These promotions weaken domestic food production and self-sufficiency, cause over-supply and price reductions through the fallacy of composition and lead to environmental degradation;
- Credit squeeze against all activities. This is deflationary, contracts the economy, reduces capacity utilization and worsens shortages of essential goods;
- Massive generalized devaluation through open foreign exchange markets, currency auctions and frequent currency depreciation. This leads to excessive increases in prices of essential goods and services, raises domestic costs of imported inputs, diverts scarce foreign exchange to speculative use, encourages capital flight, worsens income distribution, undermines growth and entrenches export of raw materials;
- High interest rates, both nominal and real, that cannot be sustained. These discourage investment, slow economic growth, make recovery difficult, fuel inflation and encourage speculative activities;
- Total import liberalization and the abolition of all import restrictions. This encourages import dumping, undermines infant industries, jeopardizes national priorities like food self-sufficiency;
- Excessive reliance on market forces for "getting prices right". This raises production costs, aggravates inflation, distorts national priorities, undermines planned development and de-rails the transformation process;

- Doctrinaire privatization of public enterprises, regardless of performance, to curb state power. This weakens the state without necessarily strengthening the indigenous private sector, facilitates foreign domination through foreign purchase of privatized enterprises, undermines industrialization of state enterprises and thereby slows the transformation process.

Alternative policy measures

In response to these measures, AAF–SAP proposes several alternative policy instruments for strengthening production, raising income, improving distribution, and changing expenditure patterns.

Production policy measures

- Land reforms – to ensure better access and entitlement to land for productive use in agriculture, industry and other sectors. This is particularly important for resolving the growing problem of landlessness among peasants, and especially women agricultural producers without traditional title to land. This is one sure way of providing opportunities for the rapid expansion of production, increase in gainful employment, general alleviation of poverty and improvement in the pattern of distribution of resources. It is also central to the economic empowerment of the people by increasing their control over their environmental resources;
- Devoting at least 20–25 per cent of total public investment to agriculture – to solve the problem of agricultural credit, improve agricultural infrastructure, (e.g., feeder roads, rural transport vehicles), raise agricultural techniques and productivity – by facilitating the acquisition of improved seed varieties and farm equipment, and increase rural employment;
- Increased foreign exchange allocation for vital imports – including agricultural and industrial inputs, employment expansion in those sectors, increased domestic production of essential commodities to avoid import strangulation and the strengthening of linkages between agriculture and industry. These are essential for the satisfaction of basic needs;
- Sectoral allocation of credit – especially through the use of credit guidelines to favour domestic food production and the manufacture of essential goods;
- Use of differential nominal interest rates – to ensure that the nominal interest rates on loans for speculative activities are higher

than rates for productive activities to promote positive weighted real interest rates for savings. This is important for the promotion of productive investment, mobilization of domestic savings, reduction of speculative activities and shifting of resources to productive activities;

- Using the existence of a *de facto* multiple exchange rate system – or the creation of such a system for essential imports, reversal of capital flight, resource mobilization and resource transfers. This is to encourage capital inflows, especially of remittances from abroad, satisfy basic needs, improve the balance of payments and to discourage capital flight;
- Establishment of a special fund for loans at subsidized interest rates for marginalized borrowers, especially in rural areas. This will encourage productive activities in selected areas;
- Creation and strengthening of rural financial institutions. This should enhance the mobilization of rural savings and improve financial intermediation;
- Promotion of small-scale industries and the use of investment codes and procedures. This will strengthen domestic production at the grassroots level, develop local enterprises, contribute to economic empowerment and the effective participation of marginalized groups in national production;
- Rehabilitation and maintenance of infrastructures – both productive and infrastructural capacities need urgent restoration and effective maintenance. These will lead to fuller capacity utilization, foreign exchange savings on the installation of new and alternative facilities and the enhancement of economic growth.

Income policy measures

The major policy measures in the African Alternative Framework for raising the aggregate level of income and improving the pattern of its distribution are:

Tax mobilization

Expansion or widening of the tax base to cover other sources of income and types of property as well as raising the efficiency and integrity of the tax collection system. These are central to increasing government revenue and eliminating the fiscal crisis of the state. They will remove the irony of the tax machinery as a cobweb that catches the fly but not the elephant – as the rich and powerful often pay little or no tax so that the distribution of the tax burden is regressive with ostentatious consumption going untaxed. The vigorous mobilization of domestic resources must thus be led by this energetic tax drive by government itself at all levels.

Drastic reduction of defence spending

African countries must urgently and drastically reduce their expenditure on defence and other non-productive public sector activities, e.g., general administration, festivals, conferences, etc. The irony of poor Africa nearly surpassing the per capita defence spending of many advanced countries must end – the slogan here is "*food not guns*". With the end of the ideological Cold War, East-West détente and the global relaxation of tensions, the atmosphere is emerging rapidly for the peaceful resolution of conflicts. This must be translated into the release of resources from unproductive defence spending for investment in directly productive activities like agriculture and industry, rehabilitation of education, health and other social services as well as the overall revamping of the economy. This will also improve resource allocation, eliminate one of the sources of the external debt crisis (i.e., foreign borrowing for imported defence gadgets) and reduce the pressure on the balance of payments.

Guaranteed minimum food prices

Minimum prices for foodstuffs should be guaranteed through the use of strategic food reserves. This is important for assuring adequate income to peasants and providing a major incentive for sustained domestic food production. This will also improve access to food for the majority of the population and more effectively control inflation caused by severe food shortages. The management of strategic food reserves for storage of surplus food during harvest periods and release of it during periods of scarcity is central to these guaranteed minimum food prices and the associated advantages.

Removal of parastatal subventions

These subventions to public enterprises should be removed except for those in the social services (education, health, etc.) and strategic basic industries like iron, steel, drugs, petro-chemicals, etc. This will force these enterprises to be self-financing, more efficient in resource use and resource generation, e.g., through the commercialization of their activities. This will remove a major source of the fiscal crisis of the state, improve fiscal balance and release resources for productive investment.

Decreasing deficit financing

Borrowing to cover budget deficits for public expenditure should be increasingly limited. To minimize foreign exchange requirements, this deficit financing should be used for productive and infrastructural investment with little import content. Consequently, these limited and decreasing budget deficits will add little to external debt and their productive investment, e.g., use for food production, will produce goods and services that people can buy. This will thus reduce the inflationary effect of such deficit financing. Deficit financing in this decreasing manner can help to sustain recovery and transformation by providing financial support for important production activities.

Expenditure policy measures.

In addition to income measures, AAF–SAP proposes specific policy instruments for improving the pattern of national expenditure to ensure the satisfaction of basic needs for food, safe drinking water, shelter, clothing, health, education and transport. These include:

Expenditure switching

Public spending should be switched – without necessarily increasing total government spending – from unproductive and defence activities to social services like education, health and the equitable integration of women into development to raise productivity and aggregate output. An average of 30 per cent of total annual government outlays should be allocated to these social services and the growth rate of public spending on these activities should exceed the annual growth rate of population. This social spending should focus on the satisfaction of critical social needs, raise investment for human resource development and thus increase living standards for the majority of the population.

Supply of essential commodities

Selective policies like subsidies, pricing rules and other incentives should be used to increase the supply of essential commodities required to meet basic needs and control inflation. This will make these essential commodities available and affordable, raise the production of intermediate and industrial raw materials, and thus increase the level of domestic production, especially in agriculture and industry.

Reduction of external debt service ratios

Payments for external debt service as a proportion of annual export earnings should be reduced to levels that permit sustained, accelerated recovery and development. This is essential to stopping external debt service from crippling domestic production and blocking the adjustment-with-transformation process. It will free resources for domestic investment and improve the balance of payments.

Selective trade policies

These include banning of some imported luxury items, high tax rates on conspicuous consumption and imported inputs when domestic substitutes are available, and mass education for the consumption of domestic goods. These are essential for changing consumption patterns, expanding markets for domestic goods, changing production patterns, internalizing the production of factor inputs and improving the balance of payments.

Selective export incentives

For processed and carefully selected raw material exports. These incentives will boost selected export commodities and encourage processing of raw materials before export. This is necessary to improve the quality and competitiveness of Africa's exports, diversify the number and range of export commodities and reduce the vulnerability of African countries to frequent and disruptive export price fluctuations. In these ways, the selective export incentives can increase the growth of exports and their earnings.

Other export promotion measures

Differential export subsidies, removal of trade barriers and encouragement of barter trade to promote intra-African trade. These will increase the diversity of export commodities, facilitate trade by removing tariff and non-tariff barriers to intra-African trade and reduce dependence on foreign exchange earnings in trade among African countries. The expansion of barter or countertrade will directly boost intra-African trade by removing the problem of export payments in so-called hard currencies or foreign exchange. In these ways, economic cooperation and integration of African countries can be sped-up to reduce excessive external dependence and vulnerability of African countries.

Bilateral and multilateral trade agreements

Agreements on primary commodities and even on non-traditional manufactured exports among African countries, on one hand, and between African countries and their foreign trade partners, on the other, are essential to expand the volume and growth of exports as well as to improve and stabilize export prices. This growth will ensure the improvement and stabilization of balance of payments.

Institutional support for recovery and transformation

The acceleration of Africa's recovery with transformation also requires institutional support in the African Alternative Framework. The proposed support includes the following:

Supervised food production credit systems

These require adequate funding for rural areas where peasants have limited access to agricultural credit due to their lack of acceptable collateral security for bank loans. Food production credit systems must thus ensure easy access to farm credit for rural cultivators through regular and supervised funding of credit schemes. These rural credit arrangements will promote sustained increases in food production and facilitate the adoption of new agricultural technologies by cultivators. One example of this is the encouragement of investments in small irrigation schemes and similar areas to reduce the vulnerability of agriculture to weather conditions.

Strengthening agricultural research

This involves focusing such agricultural research on production and preservation to reduce post-harvest losses, tying research centres more closely to agricultural producers and using agricultural extension services more widely for the diffusion and application of research results. This will facilitate Africa's agrarian revolution in five food crops that are basic to food self-sufficiency in the region, namely, maize, sorghum, millet, rice and tubers. It will also expand the production or raw materials for building a viable and sustainable industrial base.

Creation of rural industrial institutions

To support cottage and small-scale industries emphasizing indigenous technology, local finance, women's participation and rural infrastructure. These will promote rural development, make rural areas more attractive to live in, promote rural technologies, especially artisan techniques and generate rural employment to reduce the rural–urban drift.

Establishment of community development institutions

Especially NGOs and self-help programmes. These should translate the process of transformation into self-development through economic empowerment at local levels. They will tap the hidden resources of the grassroots and mobilize local knowledge and energies for community development. Direct community labour can thus be mobilized voluntarily for building rural infrastructure such as schools, health centres, feeder roads and bridges, small irrigation schemes, etc. These self-help projects are the essence of rural capital formation through the mobilization of local labour and other resources. As African countries have a long tradition of community self-help schemes, they need only to be strengthened and sustained.

Greater mass participation in programmes

Grassroots empowerment also requires the effective participation of local communities in decision-making and programme implementation. This is needed to increase the people's confidence in their own society and government, promote greater commitment and sacrifice for development and to create highly motivated human resources.

Legislative basis for ownership and participation

The encouragement of NGOs and mass participation in development requires the provision of a clear legislative or legal framework of ownership and participation by different socio-economic groups such as rural cooperatives, artisans, traders, etc. Their property and rights must be secured in law and their obligations specified to give them clear legitimacy and freedom from arbitrary harassment and uncertainty. This legal protection will promote popular participation in production, marketing, management and general development. It will also strengthen the informal sector and facilitate its integration into the formal sector and mainstream development. The point should be made here that the explosion of the informal sector in Africa, especially since the 1980s, is a consequence and reflection of the crisis, and not something to be eulogised and celebrated. Hence the need to rehabilitate those who are stranded in this bloated informal sector and facilitate their reintegration into the formal sector.

Implementation and monitoring mechanisms

AAF–SAP recognizes that the success of these policy directions and measures in achieving accelerated recovery with development depends on their effective implementation and monitoring. Hence the elaboration of the mechanisms to ensure the execution and evaluation of these alternative policies.

The mechanisms for the implementation of AAF-SAP involve (a) supplementary studies and (b) coordinated actions at national, sub-regional and international levels.

Supplementary studies

The four important supplementary studies or programmes to AAF–SAP implementation are:

African Charter for Popular Participation in Development (ACPPD) – This was produced at a major international conference of NGOs and grassroots organizations, representatives of African governments and UN agencies in Arusha, Tanzania, in February 1990 and adopted by the OAU (ECA, 1990). Its basic aim is to elaborate the framework for the effective popular participation at all levels as part of the creation of the enabling environment for the adjustment-with-transformation process. This democratization of development is essential because the implementation of AAF–SAP requires the full participation of the people in decision-making and in the implementation of projects and programmes as discussed in Chapter 6.

Selected Policy Instruments of AAF–SAP
Some major policy instruments and measures proposed in the African Alternative Framework have been studied in detail and are to be published separately as *AAF–SAP: Selected Policy Instruments*[1]. These include a multiple exchange rate system (MERS), differential interest rate policy (DIRP) with selective credit control (SCC) and price support policy for food self-sufficiency (PSP). MERS is an alternative to the unified fixed or flexible exchange rate system and includes elements of both, DIRP is an alternative to on-going unified interest rates, selective credit control recognizes the need for differentiated credit for different activities, and PSP proposes the use of selective price support policy for the encouragement of food production to achieve self-sufficiency in Africa's staple foodstuffs. The supplementary study of these policies provides the theoretical and empirical bases for each of them while offering guidelines for their design and application in different countries. These should be selectively applied according to the peculiar circumstances of each country, and following detailed studies to identify the most suitable package of policies for each country.

Popular version of AAF–SAP
To ensure its wide accessibility to the broad masses of workers, students, youths, women and politicians, AAF–SAP has been

1. ECA has a forthcoming publication on these Selected Policy Instruments.

produced in an abridged and simplified version. It is designed to become a truly political document that will animate debate at all levels of African societies and mobilize the people to take the necessary actions for its successful implementation. This is a practical way of initiating popular participation in the understanding, discussion and application of AAF–SAP itself.

Detailed country studies for the design of AAF-SAP policy packages

It is necessary for each country to use both AAF–SAP and its Selected Policy Instruments as a basis for a detailed country study in order to design its own country-specific AAF–SAP policy package. The African Alternative Framework is not a programme but a basis for the design of a programme, and its proposed policies are not to be applied indiscriminately to all countries like those of orthodox SAPs. This country study is the last step which each country has to take in order to have its own AAF–SAP based adjustment-with-transformation programme, and the study can be assisted by the ECA and the Bretton Woods institutions.

Implementation mechanisms at different levels

AAF–SAP proposes coordinated implementation mechanisms at national, sub-regional and international levels.

National level

The implementation of AAF–SAP at the national level involves the preparation of the in-depth country study as a follow-up to the *AAF–SAP Selected Policy Instruments* to formulate relevant policy packages for each country. The second stage is the actual implementation of the country-specific policy package, requiring effective social partnership between government and the people at all levels through the full democratization of decision-making and execution as well as the pragmatic coordination of public and private sectors. The specific modalities of implementation at the national level thus include:

- Preparation of the detailed national study for the formulation of a country-specific policy package for adjustment-with-transformation,
- Effective democratization of decision-making processes at national, local and grassroots levels to ensure people's full support and self-development,
- Regular and effective inter-ministerial consultations to ensure coordination of economic and social service sectors with the activities of other executive agencies and public enterprises,

- Full involvement of the national planning machinery in both design and implementation of the programme to cater adequately to long-term development,
- Consultations, cooperation and pragmatic balance between the public and private sectors to ensure full mobilization and efficient utilization of resources for the execution of programmes,
- Grassroots consultations through local authorities, community development and civic associations, including NGOs or voluntary development organizations (VDOs) to initiate a bottom-up or bottom-to-top implementation process.
- Effective popularization of national adjustment-with-transformation programmes along the lines of *Popular AAF–SAP* to fully mobilize all social forces behind the implementation process.

Sub-regional level

The implementation of AAF–SAP aims directly to arrest the growing atomization of African countries through the country-by-country approach of on-going SAPs. This requires abiding focus on the strategy of collective self-reliance as the dominant policy direction of the African Alternative Framework.

This demands the effective harmonization of adjustment policies through *sub-regional AAF-SAPs*. The critical areas of this policy harmonization include agricultural policies, fiscal and monetary policies, exchange rates, interest rates and sectoral price support. This is to avoid the neutralization of the adjustment policies of one country by the non-pursuit of similar policies by neighbouring countries. Thus the application price support policies for food production in one country alone may lead to its bumper harvest being smuggled to neighbouring countries lacking similar policies.

The needed avoidance of wasteful duplication of production units to slow increasing resource scarcity in Africa is another reason for sub-regional cooperation. Limited capital, technological, research and other resources need to be pooled to make major viable projects in industry and other activities requiring large-scale investment possible. There is also a necessity for the coordination of transport and telecommunications facilities, growing emphasis on monetary cooperation to ease payments problems, and on cooperation to arrest acute environmental threats like desertification.

The overall national adjustment-with-transformation programmes also need to be coordinated within sub-regional groupings like ECCAS, ECOWAS, PTA, etc. Indeed, these national programmes must be seen as the building blocks for the sub-regional programmes, some of whose elements must also be coordinated by institutions like ECA, MULPOCS, etc.

International level
The international community has two basic roles in the implementation of AAF-SAP. One is to accept the fact that Africans themselves must lead the process of adjustment-with-transformation. The World Bank, for example, is fond of this rhetoric – that its role is to support and not to displace the national initiative in adjustment. This must be translated into appropriate action by allowing, and even challenging, African countries to design and implement their own national programmes on the basis of the African Alternative Framework. This is the surest way of respecting the sovereignty of African countries in the adjustment process, and of ensuring the reflection of their priorities and long-term development goals in their national programmes. Of course, in the design of these alternative national programmes, the World Bank, IMF and ECA should be invited to offer advice, as well as technical and financial assistance, to the African governments.

In the second place, the international community should encourage and support the effective implementation of national programmes drawn on the basis of AAF–SAP. The support is especially necessary from the multilateral development and financial institutions and the bilateral donor agencies – to ensure that the assistance they give to African countries really generates sustained development. The NGO community, especially in the North, should put sustained pressure on their governments, the Bretton Woods institutions and related agencies to give adequate financial and technical support for the implementation of these alternative national programmes. This is urgent for arresting the widening of global disparities, the fast-growing poverty in Africa and the increasing marginalization of the region in world affairs.

Financing the implementation of AAF–SAP

The implementation mechanisms for the African Alternative Framework centre critically on the financing of the adjustment-with-transformation process. This requires the formulation of national programmes based on AAF–SAP and the determination of the resources needed for financing each national programme. In addition to the mobilization of resources discussed under the policy directions and measures, the following financing measures are necessary:

- improved commodity trade for Africa;
- effective policies and measures for the mobilization of domestic resources, e.g., rural banking and improved taxation;
- reduction of payments for external debt service from the present level of about 40 per cent of annual export earnings to a maximum of 10 per cent external debt service ratio;
- prevention of waste and financial leakages through massive capital flight, transfer pricing (especially by multinational corporations (MNCs)) and the under-declaration of export earnings;
- more efficient utilization of limited domestic resources, especially their direction from unproductive to productive use in priority economic and social sectors like agriculture and education;
- promotion of remittances and transfers home by nationals living abroad;
- generation of additional resources from the recovery and development of African economies;
- increased external resource flows from bilateral, multilateral and private foreign sources.

For example, improved commodity trade could avert situations similar to one which lost Africa $19 billion in 1985–86 through a sharp fall in export prices. The region's commodity wholesale price index at 1980 prices fell to 54.2 by 1988. Africa's foreign debt service obligations also increased to $290 billion in 1988. The annual net resource outflow from the region rose to about $5 billion during 1988–89 with a *net* transfer of $1 billion to the IMF in 1986 and 1987 (ECA, AAF-SAP, 1989, p. 52). Clearly if these perverse trends are reversed, enormous financial resources will be available for financing the implementation of programmes for adjustment-with-transformation.

Monitoring of implementation of AAF–SAP

Besides these implementation mechanisms, the African Alternative Framework provides for the systematic monitoring of programmes of adjustment-with-transformation based on AAF–SAP. Even as programmes are implemented, they often fail due to poor evaluation and monitoring, and subsequent failure to detect and correct distortions, eliminate lapses, bottlenecks and conflicts of interests as well as to sustain the morale of executing agents.

So it is necessary to assess the extent to which the objectives, targets and policies of adjustment-with-transformation programmes are being achieved – in relation to some time-table. This evaluation should be from local to national, sub-regional and regional levels so it involves the effective coordination of implementation activities at these various levels.

National governments should, therefore, establish monitoring systems appropriate for their national programmes. Such monitoring bodies should include major national agencies involved in the design and implementation processes, and should be located at the highest executive level of government to encourage and discipline erring agencies and officials. Hence Central Banks, Finance, Planning, Trade, Agriculture and related Ministries should be involved in the monitoring process, which could be an Inter-Ministerial body with full powers.

The performance indicators to be assessed should include the usual macro-economic indicators – GDP and its growth, components of aggregate demand, fiscal balance, external trade, etc. In addition, the performance indicators should focus on critical transformation variables like the impact of the programmes on quality of life in relation to the achievement of basic needs along the lines of the Human Development Index (HDI). Changes in the structures of production, consumption patterns, technology, distribution and power should be assessed equally. Such assessment should also apply to the extent of direct popular participation in the process. This can be evaluated with respect to such indices as number of women's organizations, women's enrolment, employment, leadership, similar status and the representation of socio-economic groups in decision-making bodies.

Data systems should also be developed to make the assessment as quantitative and concrete as possible. This requires systematic data collection and the revamping of statistical agencies for gathering and analysis of socio-economic data. The enhancement of capacity and training of personnel for these purposes within the framework of the national planning machinery is important.

At the sub-regional level, progress with the harmonization of fiscal, monetary, trade, agricultural, industrial and transport policies should also be monitored. This can be done through the MULPOC's (Multinational Programming and Organizational Centres) in Lusaka, Giseyin, Yaounde, Niamey and Tangiers for the sub-regional groupings. And for the whole region, the assessment of inter-country cooperation in the adjustment-with-transformation process can be done through the ECA, while the ADB can also monitor monetary and fiscal cooperation with the African Centre for Monetary Studies in Dakar.

Response to the African alternative

As would be expected in the context of the politics of adjustment, AAF–SAP has generated a very lively debate, both within and outside Africa (Adedeji, 1990, pp. 62–5). The popular and serious media have carried numerous comments and criticisms of the document and these reactions fall into two broad categories, namely, those which see nothing good in AAF–SAP and those which endorse it but see unanswered questions.

In particular, the following charges have been levelled against the document: that it constitutes no alternative to on-going orthodoxy at all; is confrontational to the Bretton Woods institutions and their major sponsors; advocates statism and dirigism; threatens current external resource mobilization for adjustment; and is not operational or feasible. Those who maintain that it is no alternative imply that on-going orthodox SAPs are divine revelation and, therefore, sacrosanct in the language of the Latin tag of medieval Christians "*Roma locuta est, causa finita est*". The ECA has also stated repeatedly that the motivation for AAF–SAP is to build consensus for the resolution of the African crisis. African Ministers of Economic Development, Planning and Finance, in their Blantyre Statement of March 1989 and Addis Ababa Joint Statement of April 1989 emphasized this need for consensus and the full support of the international community. It has also been repeated often enough that Africa's dependency is too pervasive and its economy too weak for it to seek confrontation with the Bretton Woods institutions.

The charges of statism and dirigism also seem to have arisen from pure misunderstanding. The basic position of the document is pragmatism, rather than doctrinairism, toward the roles of free market pricing, the state and private sectors. "While the Alternative is pragmatically affirmative on the role of the public sector, it is equally affirmative on the pivotal role that the private sector must play in the process of adjustment-with-transformation. The African Alternative distances itself from dirigism and dogmatic public intervention as much as from doctrinaire privatization and excessive reliance on markets and prices as allocative mechanisms. The Alternative's central aim in this area to find an objective, non-ideological balance between the public and private sectors to ensure efficiency and dynamism in national economic management. In conclusion, AAF-SAP does not advocate fat governments in Africa (what the Spanish call *estado adiposo*) but muscular government (*estado musculaso*)" (Adedeji, 1990, p. 64).

The criticism that AAF–SAP will scare foreign donors has been regarded as overt blackmail. External funding for Africa should be used purposefully to eliminate the root causes of its persistent poverty, generate fundamental structural transformation and ensure sustained development as proposed in AAF-SAP, rather than demand manipulation. Multilateral development and financial institutions as well as bilateral donors should have a vested interest in programmes that propose solutions to the ineffectiveness of their past financial assistance to Africa. Since it is generally agreed that on-going orthodox SAPs have failed to achieve their stated objective of reversing the African crisis, the funding of an alternative programme cannot objectively be said to scare external funding.

The accusation that AAF–SAP is not operational represents a misunderstanding of its nature. It is not a programme to be applied to all countries at all times, regardless of their special circumstances. Rather, it is a framework or conceptual basis for formulating national programmes from the *menu* of policy directions and measures in AAF-SAP, from which countries are to select their policy packages according to their national peculiarities. Hence the Alternative programmes will vary from country to country, and even from time to time to ensure their relevance to prevailing circumstances.

For these reasons, a more objective consideration of the African Alternative should reinforce the widespread support for it, both within and outside Africa. What is urgently required is translation of this support into practical policy actions and activities for the implementation of AAF–SAP. In this as elsewhere, absolute 100 per cent consensus is unnecessary as it is unlikely for any programme. The broad support expressed and the clarification of the outstanding questions raised should be adequate to start the practical job of implementing AAF–SAP in African countries and sub-regions.

The African Alternative Framework provides a holistic alternative to the failed on-going orthodox SAPs. Individual African countries must use it as a basis for formulating policy packages for their national adjustment-with-transformation. These should then be coordinated at sub-regional and regional levels through the effective harmonization of policies and pooling of scarce resources.

A note of warning here is a historical necessity. In 1980 the OAU prepared the *Lagos Plan of Action* (LPA) as a blueprint for Africa's development and integration up to year 2000. But the LPA was not implemented, partly because the World Bank sabotaged it with its *Berg Report* of 1981. The severity of the crisis since the 1980s would have been averted if Africa had implemented the LPA. So the question naturally arises: Has Africa learnt its lesson from that experience and resolved to implement its own programmes rather than be diverted to dead-ends by its detractors? Africa must resolve henceforth to generate the necessary self-confidence and political will to implement its own approved programmes resolutely, no matter what anybody does or says. This is the only path to wisdom and salvation for Africa – it must take its own destiny firmly in hand and occupy the driver's seat in its adjustment-with-transformation process. The recent alarming marginalization of Africa in the global economy and world affairs dictates nothing less.

Chapter 6

The necessity for democratic participation

Politics and poverty in Africa

The economism of orthodox development theory has been increasingly challenged by new conceptions of the transformation process. Apart from the mainstream development models, that emphasize such economic variables as capital, savings, trade, technology, etc., there are now three others, namely, the sociology of development, emphasizing social structure, culture and ethics; human-centred development or the human capital approach, focusing on the development of human resources; and political development which has come increasingly to stress the roles of democracy and accountability (Nyongo, 1987). These confirm the multi-faceted nature of the development process that involves all aspects of the social formation, i.e., economy, society and the state, including the ideological sphere. The persistence of underdevelopment in Africa compels greater attention to the previously neglected non-economic models of development. One example of the shift of emphasis is the 1990 UNDP *Human Development Report* (UNDP, 1990).

Another example is the increasing focus on the pervasive lack of democracy in Africa. Some in fact speak of "how politics underdevelops Africa" – much as Rodney decried *How Europe Underdeveloped Africa* (Rodney, 1972). The concern here is with the authoritarian character of the post-colonial state in Africa. The brutal, repressive apparatus of the colonial state whose mission was the subjugation of the total population under "law and order" in the interventionist bid to facilitate colonial plunder, was directly inherited by the African petty-bourgeoisie after flag independence. The broad democratic base of the anti-colonial struggle was soon subverted by the African colonial inheritors as they proceeded to Africanize colonial privileges. In the process, the promises of liberation from poverty, "life more abundant" and the satisfaction of the yearning aspirations of the people were soon betrayed. As the people watched, their hopes were dashed and their loyalty betrayed, and they mounted revolutionary pressures from below.

But the new elites would have none of that. They proclaimed the end of politics in the name of their imposed consensus on nation-building. Their narrowly based post-colonial state then replaced politics with mere administration to eliminate debate and dissent. This was associated with their ideology of containment which shifted quickly from political containment in the 1960s to repressive containment by the 1970s. The ideology of African socialism was invented by these elites to hijack the revolutionary fervour of the masses (Babu, 1981 and Gutkind and Wallerstein, 1976). The result everywhere has been widespread denial of democratic participation, pervasive one-party states, lack of accountability and the intensification of the crisis of underdevelopment from the early 1970s, which deteriorated into the continental catastrophe of a lost decade in the 1980s.

So what is basically wrong with the post-colonial state in Africa? It is repressive and authoritarian; it is not broadly based as a popular democratic state; its apparatus is over-developed relative to the fragile status of civil society and to the backward technology of the country as a whole; and it is a weak state, unable to perform the basic functions of the bourgeois state (Nyongo, 1987). The abusive and mindless political repression of the post-colonial state in Africa is both the result of its inherited colonial authoritarianism and the consequence of its need to suppress popular demands for a higher standard of living, effective political competition and a broad basis of governance that it cannot accommodate. So it finds it easier to engage in the coercive containment of these legitimate demands than to transform society and ensure a better life.

The unpopular and narrow political base of the African state is also due to the exploitative alliance of the African petty-bourgeoisie and the imported or foreign oligarchy of representatives of the imperial estate from the West and their multinational corporations. Whether civilian or military, it is basically the same cliques in power – local and foreign representatives of dominant classes. Their common platform is the preservation and strengthening of the structures – economic, political and social – that protect and guarantee their vital economic interests, control of political power and exclusive privileges. In francophone Africa, the French have simply refused to decolonize effectively by maintaining physical control of vital organs of the state and economy in alliance with a tiny national minority. They maintain stifling and one-sided defence agreements with the francophone countries, station the largest number of troops all over Africa, trap these countries into the *franc unìon* with France in the

CFA Zone[1] and still directly own and control most economic enterprises in these countries, from bars or cafés to industries. So even the modest indigenization of foreign enterprises in the rest of Africa has not been tolerated by the French – as they systematically sabotage and undermine economic cooperation and integration among African countries which directly threatens their vicious control and exploitation of them.

The relative weakness of civil society in Africa also reinforces the pervasiveness of the state and its authoritarian character. Countervailing forces to the state such as religious organizations, trade unions, peasant organizations, student movements, women's organizations, NGOs, civic groups and similar voluntary associations either do not exist or are very weak. This is in sharp contrast to the prolific growth, enormous resources and impressive strength of these mass organizations in the advanced countries. Usually, the stronger these organs of civil society, the greater their capacity to act as checks and balances, or as a counterweight to the excesses of state and power and its organs. This relative weakness of civil society increases the *relative autonomy of the post-colonial state* in the region (Poulantzas, 1975 and Alavi, 1972). But by forcing the state to become the focus of most social antagonisms and national struggles, this weakness of civil society undermines the resilience and strength of the state (political and moral) by exposing its mystique to more frequent controversies and conflicts.

In the fourth place, the post-colonial state in Africa, like those elsewhere in the Third World, is relatively weaker than its counterpart in the developed countries. This is especially with respect to its executive capacity to perform the statutory or conventional functions of the state. Even as interventionist state bureaucratic capitalism (SBC), this post-colonial state is unable to ensure elemental security of life and property, maintain durable civic order, provide the basic needs of the population like food, safe drinking water, health care, education, housing, sewage disposal and transport. This is not to mention achieving the goals of national economic management such as full or high level employment, satisfactory growth rate,price stability, rising standard of living and the alleviation of poverty. Indeed, the repressive and authoritarian disposition of the post-colonial state seems inversely proportional to its failure and inability to perform its basic functions. All these make the transformation of the post-colonial

1. The 12 members of the CFA Zone are Cote d'Ivoire, Senegal, Mali, Cameroon, Congo, Togo, Benin, Gabon, Chad, Niger, Central African Republic and Burkina Faso.

state in Africa an urgent necessity.

The *World Democratic Revolution* has unfolded, especially since the late 1980s, and the reforms in Eastern Europe have already started to effect several African countries, especially those under one-party rule. Everywhere, the basic demands of this world democratic movement are the same – opening up of the state, respect for human rights, people's participation, political and economic empowerment, effective accountability and greater control by the people over their own lives. In Africa, these demands also include the termination of sit-tight regimes and the changing of leaders who have stood for office for over 20 years since flag independence. The "small cliques in power" are being challenged by the popular masses. A new "wind of change" is blowing across Africa.

Western countries have been supporting this world democratic upsurge, perhaps, because they see it as a triumph of their democratic model and ideal. They have discreetly approved and modestly supported the democratic movements and demands for the end of one-party rule in some African countries. The North-South Dialogue or European Roundtable organized by the Council of Europe has been particularly helpful to this democratic upsurge in Africa.[2] But there are differences between the democratic perspectives of the Western countries and those of Africa. For the West, the basic concern is with multi-party (or better still two-party) parliamentary democracy with periodic elections.

African countries are asking for more – in addition to multi-party rule, not just two-party elections, they demand the immediate stepping-down of sit-tight leaders to institutionalize periodic and peaceful succession of leadership, effective popular participation of all social groups – workers, peasants, women, youths, students, professionals and the poor in both urban and rural areas. Participation is sought in decision-making and resource allocation at all levels from grassroots to the government, especially by the weak and poor, through the democratization of access to the means of production (land, credit, facilities, etc.), equitable distribution of the benefits of development, and effective accountability of leadership at all levels, both financially and politically. Urgent steps must be taken for the alleviation and eventual termination of the abusive and growing

---

2. This North-South Dialogue was held in Port-Novo, Benin Republic in August 1988 and in Dakar during March 25–26, 1991 on the theme "Democracy and Development in Africa – the Experience of the African ACP Countries" under the auspices of the Strasbourg Conference on Parliamentary Democracy.

poverty and misery of the majority of the population – often in the midst of revolting and scandalous displays of corrupt wealth by the parasitic petty-bourgeoisie.

Experience with democratic constitutions in post-colonial Africa has shown that without these entrenched commitments to popular participation and empowerment of the people, political pluralism can easily be rigged into a sham. Thus unless immensely unequal distribution of income, wealth and power can be changed, multi-party democracy is soon cornered by "money-bags" (as the corrupt rich are called in Nigeria) as Adam Smith feared when he stated in *The Wealth of Nations*:

> Till there be property, there can be no government, the very end of which is to secure wealth, and to protect the rich from the poor.

So political democracy cannot go far without the effective democratization or redistribution of economic power. This is because *freedom and choice* (and hence debate) which lie at the heart of democracy pre-suppose the *means* of exercising them. African masses have long recognized the futility of asking a starving, unemployed illiterate to exercise freedom of speech in English and choose between party programmes – the first choice is the stomach and then other basic needs. This is how the rich and powerful everywhere, including the West, dominate all political and even multi- or two-party democratic processes because:

> Power and property may be separated for a while by force or fraud, but divorced never; For as soon as the pang of separation is felt, property will purchase power, or power will take over property. And either way, there must be an end to free government. (Benjamin Watkin Leigh).

Hence equitable democratic participation in the development process and its benefits must be the heart of the on-going democratic upsurge across Africa.

Democracy, accountability, peace and development

The drive for full democratization of African societies is aimed at ensuring popular participation through the restructuring of the post-colonial state. But these are also means to three basic ends, which are the achievement of effective accountability, durable peace and accelerated adjustment-with-transformation. In whatever terms these are defined, establishment of democracy is essential to their realization. These goals used to be regarded as a trilogy – democracy, accountability and development (DAD), but it is well to add the fourth critical element of domestic peace, though it is implied by the others. The logical interrelationship of these four requirements in the African development equation is compelling. Without democracy, there can be no effective accountability; without democratic participation, accountability, social justice or equity, there can be no lasting peace and no end to pervasive conflicts and strife within and between African countries; and without accountability and peace, no sustainable development is possible.

Democracy and accountability

With widespread abuse of power at all levels in African countries, the need for both political and financial accountability is very high on the political agenda. But what is not so familiar is the fact that this accountability has been elusive because there has been no democracy. In particular, cynical political leaders have trivially equated accountability with the declaration of assets of ministers and other political leaders in secret on assumption of office – and in some cases, with periodic statements of their stewardship to the media. This is the manipulation of accountability that must be a participatory two-way process between government and governed. So it is not enough to call ministers behind closed doors to declare their assets to presidents and the President to declare his before the Chief Justice. On leaving office, the Ministers and presidents also declare their assets in private. We are not impressed by this farcical asset declaration which leaves us uninformed. We want to know what assets are declared, why it is not public, since these leaders are public officials and sworn-in publicly, and how these declared assets are verified, especially when leaders leave office? If this asset declaration is honest, how is it that these presidents, ministers, etc. amass enormous wealth running into millions and billions of dollars after a few years in office? Making self-congratulatory statements of stewardship to the press in the name of accountability is also cynical because the procedure involves little direct participation by the people, there is no verification and there are no sanctions for official failure. Indeed, the reverse often holds, and the most unpopular ministers often get promoted to bigger ministries in obvious disdain for the discontent of the people.

So what is accountability in the context of democracy? Its objectives are to ensure that: (a) public resources and property are effectively protected – not swindled – and that these resources are utilized efficiently according to popularly determined national priorities; (b) the loyalty of the people to their government is not betrayed through the abuse of power; (c) as "power corrupts and absolute power corrupts absolutely", that checks and balances are maintained; and (d) a decent moral tone of government is maintained to prevent official corruption.

To achieve these goals, accountability must include the following basic elements:

Financial and political accountability

Public officials must account fully for money and other public resources or property entrusted to their care, and be accountable for their policy decisions, measures, actions or inaction. The open declaration of assets, both before and after taking office, deals partly with financial accountability, while periodic statements of official stewardship deal partly with political accountability. The late President Sankara of Burkina Faso was said to have declared his assets publicly to his countrymen and women before taking office – he was not allowed to do so on leaving office. In addition to open asset declaration, public accounts must be audited regularly (annually) by internal and external auditors and auditors' queries must be fully answered by officials at all levels. A situation in which the accounts of Ministries, Departments, parastatals and even whole governments are not audited regularly is a violation of this procedure. Those who are found guilty of swindling public funds or property must not just be retired or dismissed from public service – they must face the full rigour of the law by being openly prosecuted and compelled to make full restitution or refund before being jailed or dismissed. In Ethiopia, it is said that officials who embezzle public property are forced to refund it before being jailed for some years. So financial accountability involves open declaration of assets on taking and leaving office, regular internal and external audit of public accounts at all levels, prompt replies to auditors queries, and due punishment for those who swindle public funds and property. The pervasive lack of this financial accountability accounts for much of the stinking official corruption in Africa and for about 50 per cent of the financial crisis facing many countries. Thus if about 50 per cent of the flight or stipendiary capital swindled and stacked abroad in foreign secret bank accounts from these countries can be recovered, much of their financial crisis will be greatly eased.

Political accountability also involves public officials living by their oath of office and being accountable to the public for their decisions, actions and inaction. Hence the oath of officials must be binding. In traditional African societies, officials swore by gods or deities and those who violated such oaths were visited with swift punishment, including death. Thus in Western Nigeria, people traditionally swore by *Ogun*, the god of iron, or by *Sango*, the god of thunder, and those who violated such oaths faced swift punishment. But these days, people swear on bibles and korans only to violate their oath of office with impunity. Political accountability also includes public accounts of stewardship to the general public – not just the media – and people must be free during those sessions to raise queries and seek redress for wrong-doing. More importantly, aggrieved citizens must get fairly prompt redress – either through bureaucratic/administrative channels or from the courts. Hence the rule of law must be binding under an independent and incorruptible judiciary to enforce political accountability. Leaders and officials who abuse their power must be removed from office. Open public debate of policies is essential to enlist popular participation in the choice of priorities for policy at all levels of government. Where this debate is stifled, there cannot be political accountability. Where a Public Complaints Commission exists as in Nigeria, it must function openly and have disciplinary powers if it is not to become a cynical cover for the abuse of power.

Effective sanctions

Any system of accountability must be accompanied by binding sanctions to be effective. Leaders, policy-makers and other officials who violate their oath of office, swindle public funds or property, or abuse their power must be tried and punished openly. Thus it is wrong for officials who are accused of wrong-doing to be 'investigated' secretly and then cleared by other officials as is the case in many countries. This is plain corruption, abuse of power and an insult to the public. Clear administrative, audit and legal procedures should exist for the investigation and discipline of leaders and officials at all levels, and these must be enforced – in the full view of the public. Justice must not only be said to be done, it must *be seen* by the general public to be done. So erring officials and leaders must be tried openly and punished effectively, no matter their rank or office – from the President to the messenger. Public hearings must also be instituted. The removal of Richard Nixon as President of the USA in the Watergate episode (because he manipulated the electoral process) thus stands supremely as a shining example of political accountability. Part of the tragedy of Africa is that leaders and officials rarely have the honour to resign and receive no effective punishment – according to specified procedures – when they violate their oath of office. If Africa is to catch up with the rest of the world, this bogus, hypocritical and corrupt situation must change urgently. People must accept and be made to take full responsibility for their actions – no matter how highly placed they may be. Officials and leaders who perform brilliantly should also be rewarded, e.g., with national awards.

Popular participation

To have effective accountability, there must be democratic participation in decision-making and execution at all levels of government. This starts with *the right to know and to be informed* – the people must know what government, leaders and officials are doing on their behalf. Bogus colonial secrecy laws according to which virtually all files and documents are marked 'secret' must be jettisoned for this purpose. These colonial secrecy laws were designed to *protect* colonial predators from accountability and that cannot hold in the post-colonial era. Freedom of speech and of the press with investigative journalism are also required. People as citizens must reserve the inalienable right to criticize government, policies, leaders and officials – without precondition to "constructive" criticism as is often demanded by leaders. "We welcome criticism but it must be constructive, responsible and informed". Who determines when criticism satisfies these pre-conditions? We insist that criticism must be general and uninhibited – if people criticize wrongly in a way that breaks the law, let them be prosecuted.

The people must also be free to take part in decision-making at all levels of government. This is the surest way to prevent arbitrary and wrong decisions because "two heads are better than one". Moreover, if the people themselves participate in decision-making through debate, public discussion and by attending meetings, they will contribute their knowledge and be aware of violations by leaders and officials.

Through popular participation, people exercise greater control over their lives and environment. This diminishes the scope of official intervention and reduces the chances of abuse of power. Democratic participation also ensures greater public control over the allocation of resources, and this reduces the opportunity for official corruption. By ensuring political and economic empowerment – with the freedom of assembly and association – people develop self confidence and are able to demand and enforce accountability on their leaders and officials. Conversely, if people are excluded from participation at all levels of government, they can hardly know when oaths of office are violated, the redress for this, or how to pursue it.

When the people in mass organizations and local associations participate in government as *groups*, they compel more attention from leaders and officials. They can host meetings, symposia, etc. to which they can invite officials for open dialogue. Disputed policies and procedures can be discussed in such forums. Representatives of these mass organizations and NGOs can also link up with media as watchdogs of the democratic process as, "eternal vigilance is the price of liberty". This popular participation is the surest means of enlarging civil society as a check on excessive government.

Open accountability

Financial and political accountability must be clearly visible by the general public. Hence accountability requires *open government* – through unfettered public debate, free press, free speech and the right to a fair public hearing. When assets are declared secretly, stewardship is rendered to a select few, and punishment is not open, accountability is jeopardized.

The public must be allowed to scrutinize published accounts, acquire external auditors' reports and follow investigations of wrongdoing by officials. In the process, the public can defend leaders and officials that have been wrongly accused, and demand punishment for those convicted. Public hearings on specific policies and questions of probity should also be held regularly in designated places.

Open accountability will enhance the confidence of the people and their loyalty to government, leaders and officials. Accountability procedures also promote civic responsibility and education. Conversely, secrecy in the conduct of public affairs breeds suspicion, rumours and disinformation which destroy confidence in any government, no matter how good its actions or intentions may be.

Investigation

To be effective, accountability procedures must also be investigative. The facts of financial and policy controversies need to be known. External auditors' reports are standard examples of this investigative role. Good journalism backed by research (library and empirical) supports such investigation.

When leaders and officials are accused of violating their oath, impartial investigation should be promptly undertaken. Members of the public could be invited to participate in such investigations. Public hearings can help ascertain the facts of each case objectively and fairly. Firm and adequate disciplinary action should then be taken.

Accountability, peace and development

The move to transcend economism in the development dialogue must incorporate the critical roles of accountability and peace into the process of Africa's transformation. The horrendous damage to the region's development caused by lack of both are enough to warrant this. In addition to the enormous corrupt siphoning of resources, widespread strife and conflicts have also been major setbacks for development. These have led to massive destruction of life and property, e.g. Angola is reported to have lost around $20 billion from the destruction of property in its civil war. Countries like Chad, Mozambique, Ethiopia, Somalia, Uganda, Sudan, Rwanda and Liberia, have effectively ground to a halt due to internal strife.

The appalling and growing refugee problem is a by-product of this pervasive strife across Africa (Cimade *et al.*, 1986). Most of these political and economic refugees are the hapless victims of civil wars, border clashes and similar conflicts. Africa's staggering annual expenditure of over 10 per cent of total government spending on defence in many countries is solidified by these sporadic domestic conflicts. Estimated at billions of dollars per annum, these arms expenditures represent the diversion of sizeable portions of Africa's limited and dwindling resources. The debilitating insecurity, fear and uncertainty caused by these conflicts prevent or militate against sustained economic activity.

Unfortunately, the denial of democracy and equitable popular participation in development is often at the root of these internal conflicts. The major causes include ethnicity, or the ethnic monopoly of power, that denies pluralism; one-party rule and the marginalization of opposition groups; sit-tight leadership with the denial of leadership succession. There are other factors, but the elimination of these through effective democratization will restore a great deal of the peace so critical to development.

The roles of democracy, accountability and peace (DAP) in development hinge critically on popular participation. The denial of democratic rights and people's participation at all levels of government is a major source of the sporadic lack of accountability and peace in Africa. When the people are marginalized, and even alienated from government and leaders, their confidence is seriously eroded. Government then becomes an affair for small cliques, shielding their abuse of power with secrecy. Enormous resources are swindled with impunity and the development process is correspondingly starved of funds. In addition, public morale is severely undermined, the work ethos come under attack, and productivity drops as honest people watch helplessly while corruption catapults crooks and idiots into instant wealth. This lack of accountability also causes systematic distortion of development priorities, the diversion of those resources that escape embezzlement into unproductive ventures and the non-implementation of projects and policies as leaders and officials become increasingly unaccountable. The absence of democracy in African countries has encouraged a lack of accountability, and generated conflicts and strife, throttling the adjustment and development process.

African Charter for Popular Participation

To overcome these political failures and contribute to the creation of an enabling environment for development, the ECA coordinated a joint conference of NGOs in Africa and the North, government representatives, and the UN in Arusha, Tanzania in February 1990. It produced the *African Charter for Popular Participation in Development* (ACPPD) which as been adopted by the OAU. The Charter was motivated by the feeling that though Africa missed the Renaissance, the Reformation and the Industrial Revolution, it must not miss the on-going World Democratic Revolution. The people themselves must seize the initiative and recast history in their own popular image. They must join the rest of humanity in Eastern Europe, Asia and elsewhere to open African societies and governments, demand the enforcement of democratic rights that governments have ratified, and enthrone people's participation as the basic organizational principle for the pursuit of accelerated recovery with sustainable development in Africa. Only if, and when, the people effectively seize control of the dynamics of the transformation process can genuine development be realized and become self-sustaining.

The charter is a follow-up to the *African Alternative Framework* (AAF-SAP) and one of the mechanisms for its implementation. It details an aspect of the requirements for the creation of an enabling environment for adjustment with transformation. One of the policy directions in AAF-SAP is the creation of a conducive atmosphere that will encourage the democratic participation required for mobilizing domestic resources, executing policies and projects and equitable sharing of the benefits of development.

Main features of the African Charter

A major feature of the African Charter for Popular Participation (ACPPD) is the idea of a *new partnership between government and the people*. The participation of government officials in the preparation of the Charter and its adoption by the OAU underscores this new partnership. Government must yield political and social space to enable the popular forces of workers, peasants, women, youths, students and professionals to participate more actively in the adjustment with development process. This is the surest way of translating people-centred development into practical reality. People are both the central means and the end of the adjustment-with-development process. Their resources, energies, talents and local knowledge must be fully mobilized if development is to occur, and conversely, if this lack of democratic participation continues, so will the stifling of recovery and development across Africa. As the end of the development process, satisfaction of people's basic needs must be a major objective of adjustment-with-transformation. People of all strata of society must share equitably in the benefits of development through the development of their human resources and the steady increase of their living standard.

The ACPPD also prescribes participatory roles for government and different social groups in the process of adjustment-with-development. Thus it contains sections on the responsibilities of government, NGOs, workers and their trade unions, peasants, women, youths and students. As the government leads and coordinates the entire development process, it must also accommodate the equitable participation of the people in social groups and mass organizations. The NGOs or voluntary development organizations (VDOs) – as African NGOs are called to avoid any notion of confrontation with authority for being non-governmental (and, therefore, anti-governmental) – must become better organized at local, national, subregional and regional levels. Thus the Pan-African VDO (PAVDO) is a federation of African VDOs with umbrella national VDOs as constituent members. These NGOs and VDOs themselves must become more democratic and accountable to be more effective in propelling bottom-to-top development. The trade unions should be given a free hand to organize, and governments should implement ILO conventions on workers' and trade union rights in their respective countries. Trade unions must also assist the process of organizing peasants to defend their rights and contribute more effectively to adjustment-with-transformation. Youths and students as future leaders must be given the best education through better funding and security from harassment, dismissal, and closure of educational institutions.

The Charter also reinforces the position of the Fourth ECA Regional Conference in Abuja, Nigeria, in November 1989 on the *Integration of Women in Development in Africa* which affirmed that:

> until we have realized the goal of fully integrating women in the development process, our effort to bring about a fundamental transformation of our economies, of our societies and of our policies will continue to be frustrated. How can we ever hope to achieve an economic breakthrough and maximize our production possibilities when half of our population are, on account of their gender, not enabled by the society to contribute optimally in accordance with their abilities? How can we unleash our creative energies when half of our population remains constrained? (Adedeji, 1989 p. 107).

The equal education, employment and development of women is, therefore, imperative with full access to land, credit and other productive resources for them. On their part, women have to organize more effectively (especially rural women who need urban assistance to do so), in democratic and accountable organizations to participate more fully and equitably in development.

In these ways, the African Charter on Popular Participation underscores the critical differences between the African democratic movement and the Western model of democracy. Thus, social groups and their mass organizations are critical foci in the democratization process and imply the implementation of basic democratic rights for individuals. People's economic and political empowerment is thus a major component of the African agenda. These are basic predicates for the success of multi-party (not just two-party as in the Western democratic ideal) democracy. In particular, the democratization of economic power through the redistribution of income and wealth is crucial for the successful exercise of fundamental human rights, e.g., freedom of speech in English or French is useless to an illiterate, just as other democratic freedoms are not particularly appealing to a starving person.

Response to the African Charter

Since the Arusha Conference, the response to the African Charter for Popular Participation (ACPPD) has been very enthusiastic, both within and outside Africa. The adoption of the Charter by the OAU member states is a very positive development in this respect. This is despite the doubts of many about the seriousness of African countries to democratize and about their willingness to implement the Charter. But as the Chinese say, even "a thousand mile journey must start with the first step". That the OAU could adopt a charter on popular participation by workers, peasants, women, youths and students in the face of the pervasive lack of democracy in Africa, is a very encouraging step forward.

The implementation of the Charter by African governments depends partly on them, partly on the African masses themselves and partly on the unfolding trend of the World Democratic Revolution. In spite of continuing strong resistance to democratization in many African countries, as reflected by the spate of pro-democracy riots across the region, some countries have already begun cautious implementation of the Charter. Thus countries like Benin and Mali have already replaced their dictatorships, and Gabon has held a multi-party election since the adoption of the Charter in 1990. Other countries like Zambia, Zaire, Cote d'Ivoire and Togo have agreed to modify their one-party government by allowing opposition parties to organize. In a few of the other countries like Cameroon and Kenya, the government is still sticking to one-party rule. But it is evident that the "new wind of change" that has been blowing across Africa since 1990 is gathering momentum. Some even see a hurricane already with the rapid collapse of the dictatorships in Liberia, Chad, Somalia, Mali and Benin in quick succession within one year from 1990. These changes can indeed be taken to herald "the second coming of Africa". But much remains to be done to achieve the objectives of ACPPD and fully democratize African societies.

Many Africans have already warmly embraced the African Charter. Most of them, their NGOs and grassroots organizations see the Charter as a major political blueprint around which to organize their campaigns and for which they must mobilize and struggle. Thus the organization of African Trade Union Unity (OATUU) organized a joint regional conference with ECA on Popular Participation and AAF-SAP in Addis Ababa, Ethiopia, in March 1992. A network of environmental NGOs in West Africa are also planning an international conference on Popular Participation and the Environment in Lagos, Nigeria, during the first half of 1992. Similar conferences have been organized by different NGOs and grassroots organizations on the themes of democratization and recovery across Africa.

At the international level, the African Charter has been very warmly received by governments, multilateral institutions, the UN system,

NGOs and grassroots organizations. The Charter has been distributed widely in Europe and North America, given wide media coverage in both the popular and serious press there, and animated and contributed to a lively dialogue between Africa and the world community on the democratization process. Since the adoption of ACPPD, the Council of Europe has held conferences in Africa under the auspices of the Strasbourg Conference on Parliamentary Democracy. The Bretton Woods institutions have hailed the Charter as a major development toward the creation of an enabling environment for recovery-with-transformation.

Commentaries and discussions of the African Charter for Popular Participation, however, emphasize the question of implementation machinery. This is against the background of doubts that have been raised, both inside and outside Africa, about the seriousness and sincerity of African governments in their adoption of the Charter. In addition to the empirical implementation of the Charter that has been mentioned, the ACPPD itself addresses the issues of implementation and evaluation.

Implementation and monitoring of popular participation

The implementation and monitoring of popular participation in adjustment-with-transformation is primarily the joint responsibility of the African people and their governments. But the international community, especially Western governments and the UN system, also have important roles to play. Within the continent, the requisite modalities must be applied at national and regional levels.

National and regional implementation

At the national and regional levels, governments must increasingly see the necessity for democratic participation in the adjustment-with-transformation process. This is partly because the bulk of economic activities such as production and investment are carried on by people at the local level. The vigorous mobilization of domestic resources and their efficient allocation is impossible without the active participation of the people in creating savings, changing consumption habits, developing banking habits, especially in rural areas, and contributing their talents and knowledge. The energies of the people are also required for the execution of development projects. To achieve these, the people must be equitably rewarded through the fair distribution of the benefits of development. Similarly, African governments must correctly perceive the democratic wind of change in Africa and bend with it. They must correctly learn the lessons of the democratic reforms in Eastern Europe, especially the bitter and pointless resistance in Romania, and initiate necessary reforms before it is too late. As history unfolds, the people will never lose, especially if they are mobilized. By honourably adopting ACPPD, African governments should put the necessary machinery in motion for implementing it at all levels of society. They must see the need for this new social partnership in development and yield space for it.

They must open up their one-party governments by allowing opposition groups to organize and contest elections freely, with sit-tight leaders yielding voluntarily to leadership succession before being pushed out. They must implement the *African Charter on Human and People's Rights* which they have ratified – this is the path of honour. This implies granting freedom of association for workers, NGOs and grassroots and popular organization of trade unions and similar mass organizations. They must also implement the trade union rights they ratified in the ILO Convention and implement the UN Charter on Women's Rights along with the *Abuja Declaration on Women* by African countries. They must realize that it is impossible to transform Africa without the active and equitable participation of women who constitute half of the population. At the regional level, the OAU must continue to offer leadership by endorsing democratic participation and urging member states to implement it. The OAU's mediation organ must also be more active and effective in internal conflicts over popular participation.

The primary responsibility for the implementation of popular participation lies with the broad masses themselves. They must seize the initiative, and *organize* to mount a militant and uncompromising demand for democratization. Popular participation is basically a *group* phenomenon and so organization into associations and democratic movements is crucial. The people must recognize their own potential and capacity to enforce democratic participation. This self-confidence is essential for success and should be disseminated widely among the people at all levels in both urban and rural areas.

Mass political education is central to sustained democratic mobilization. Trade Unions, NGOs, Women, Peasant and Youth organizations must, therefore, conduct political education for their members to raise their political consciousness. This includes education about the democratic rights of citizens, nature of parliamentary democracy, operation of political parties and elections as well as the *patriotic duties of citizens* to uphold the constitution, demand due process and the rule of law, protect public resources and property by exposing official corruption, e.g. holding meetings, keeping minutes, raising funds, keeping financial records, etc. The mass media have a vital role to play in this so that the masses can also join the media to defend the freedom of the press. Civil liberties organizations and similar bodies should also be created to promote political education, defend democratic rights and encourage people's participation. Trade unions must also mobilize their members to participate fully in politics by forming their own political parties.

This role of the people in the democratization process also includes *networking and the formation of broad-based democratic alliances*. Thus a National *Democratic Alliance or Front* has to be established as an umbrella organization to unite the different people's organizations – trade unions, peasant associations, women, youth, students and professional organizations. This unity is their strength for bargaining effectively with government on democratic participation. The trade unions, NGOs, women and students' movements, in particular, must learn the techniques of *networking* – forming links among themselves, supporting each other's activities, exchanging information, etc., without necessarily losing their separate identities. The absence of these networks is one of the main weaknesses of mass organizations and NGOs in Africa. In addition to national networks, sub-regional and regional networks of people's organizations from the grassroots level upward is essential for the exchange of information about political developments in different countries, mutual support, broadening of knowledge and experiences in political education and for sheer strength. Thus the Pan-African Voluntary Development Organization (PAVDO) need to be strengthened for consultation and bargaining with national governments and the OAU. The OATUU has been doing this effectively on behalf of African workers and trade unions, especially since the 1980s. Other Pan-African organizations like IFAA, AAPS, CODFSRIA, AFEA, etc. should give their intellectual support to people's organizations and join in the demand for effective popular participation for recovery and transformation in Africa.

The international role

The international role in the pursuit of democratic participation in Africa is very important in four areas. One is the urgent termination of the economic, military and political support of Western governments for maintaining several dictators across Africa. The militarization of politics through the staging of unpopular military coups against elected governments, and the direct Western support for installing and maintaining dictators in many African countries must stop. It is a betrayal of the democratic struggles and gains of African people, a gross violation of their sovereignty and a hypocritical and cynical act of double standard. The Western governments cherish and promote democracy in their own countries and so have absolutely no moral right to install, aid or abett dictatorship and the subversion of the democratic process in African countries. African people demand its end. The Council of Europe, under its Strasbourg Conference on Parliamentary Democracy, should also join hands with the African masses to tell their governments in Europe and North America to stop their highly unpopular support for dictators who systematically undermine democracy in Africa. In Benin Republic, a beginning has been made but much remains to be done.

Foreign aid is a powerful weapon that can be used for this international support for democracy against dictatorship in Africa. Some call it democratic conditionality but it does not have to go that far – because this conditionality can also be abused to undermine the sovereignty of African countries. In subtle and discreet ways, distinct hints can be dropped that unless governments open up for democratic participation, they will not continue to receive Western aid. Japan and other countries should add their powerful economic might behind this support for the democratization process in Africa. Happily some action is being taken by some Western governments along these lines against some undemocratic regimes in Africa – but the scope of this should be greatly widened to speed full democratization.

Northern NGOs and popular lobbies that have shown immense solidarity with African people since the crisis in the 1980s also have a role to play in this democratic movement. They can mount pressures on, and expose the duplicity of, their governments that install and support dictatorial regimes in African countries. Amnesty International should do more than list violations of human rights in the region – it should also expose the Western governments whose support and tacit approval facilitates these gross violations of democratic rights and the undermining of popular participation. This northern solidarity has been very effective in averting absolute catastrophe during the crisis of the 1980s, and it should be extended to the support of democratic struggles in the region. The major reason why northern governments, institutions and NGOs should actively support the democratic movement in Africa is that their aid fatigue and the ineffectiveness of their past assistance to African countries has been due in large measure to lack of democracy and effective accountability. Therefore they should support popular participation to promote recovery-with-transformation so that this aid can become more productive and promote the capacity of African countries to become self-sustaining, and thus reduce their demand for foreign aid.

The international community can also perform an effective job of exposing and fighting violations of democratic rights in African countries. By reporting these attacks on democratic participation, defending the rights of political prisoners (or prisoners of conscience), attending their trials and monitoring elections, this international solidarity constitutes great diplomatic and moral pressure against democratic abuse in Africa. The World Democratic Movement should become truly international and supported globally to make life difficult for dictators and enemies of democracy everywhere.

Monitoring the progress of popular participation

To ensure its effective implementation and sustenance, the extent of democratic participation must be continuously assessed. The African Charter for Popular Participation provides for this monitoring at national, regional and international levels.

This requires identification of the *performance criteria* to be assessed and the monitoring mechanisms to be used. Some of the suggested criteria include the number of political parties, trade unions, NGOs and other mass organizations in each country; their membership, especially of trade unions; the status of women with respect to education, environment, employment, executive positions, access to land and credit; and the major violations of democratic rights such as number of political prisoners, closure of educational institutions, etc. Periodic reports can be provided on these criteria by some NGOs or even governments to reflect the progress of democratic participation.

The specific monitoring mechanisms can then include bodies like *Africa Watch* (both an organization and a periodic publication), Amnesty International, etc. But Amnesty International should also report democratic violations, especially against racial minorities in Western countries, and not concentrate only on Third World countries. Similar democratic-watch bodies like civil liberties organizations should be formed in each country, and these watch groups should network at national, sub-regional, regional and international levels for better information and coverage. National and regional bar associations like the African Bar Association (ABA) and the League of Democratic Lawyers should be actively involved in this monitoring function. Funds and legal assistance should be mobilized to facilitate these activities. The OAU should also monitor the implementation of democratic participation in African countries and issue periodic reports on its assessment. This should be seen as part of its activity for the control of internal conflicts and strife, which often arise from democratic denial and abuse. The annual survey of economic and social conditions in Africa by the ECA can also report on the achievement of the performance criteria of popular participation. This evaluation of democratic participation by the OAU and ECA, with possible financial assistance from the ADB, should be seen as an integral component for monitoring the progress of adjustment-with-transformation in African countries.

Chapter 7
Transcending the politics of adjustment

Transcending the politics of adjustment that has raged since the 1980s involves summing up the debate and the lessons that have been learnt, underlining the areas of agreement and translating the conclusions from the debate into concrete policy actions and programmes for resolving the crisis that called for adjustment in the first place. It is another way of demanding that we apply the knowledge gained from the debate to move the African agenda forward. It is a demand that we must move from scoring debating points into the realm of concrete action to terminate the loss of time and opportunities that Africa has suffered since the 1980s. A note of caution here: transcending the adjustment debate must not become an intolerant demand to replace adjustment politics with adjustment administration in a false claim that the options, goals and instrumentalities of adjustment have been settled. Rather, it is to shift the focus of the debate to policy actions, while disagreements shift more to implementation mechanisms and practical options for resolving the crisis. Africa cannot adjust indefinitely – it must resume its growth and transformation in the 1990s simultaneous to the pursuit of recovery.

Hence transcending the politics of adjustment requires the explicit recognition of the objective limitations of the adjustment process to date; taking stock of the lessons from the experience of the 1980s; summarizing and building on the consensus that has arisen from the adjustment debate; dealing with the question of adjustment, transformation and delinking or structural disengagement; and the concrete formulation and implementation of a development agenda for Africa in the 1990s.

Objective limitations of adjustment

Many detailed studies and publications have provided empirical and scientific evaluations of on-going orthodox adjustment programmes as discussed in Chapter 4. They include the reports of the World Bank,

UNICEF, ILO, UNDP, ECA, IFAA, the Commonwealth Office, and other international and regional organizations. Individually and collectively, these studies, reports and publications show that orthodox adjustment has been a disastrous failure, even a catastrophe in human terms – in the 34 African countries that have been forced to adopt these SAPs. Thus in 1981, 21 African countries were among the least developed countries (LDCs), but by 1990, their number had risen to 29. Their external debt and debt-servicing rose to $203.9 per person while their income was barely $221.4 per capita. Nigeria, Ghana, Liberia, Zambia, Equatorial Guinea and Sao Tome fell from middle-income to low-income status during their operation of SAPs in the 1980s. Despite improved agricultural performance, FAO estimated cereal import requirements for sub-Saharan Africa at 8.2 million tons, with 3.8 million tons to be covered by food aid in 1989. GDP growth rate varied from 1.7 per cent to 2.3 per cent during 1987–88, and even by 1990 remained below the population growth rate of 3.0 per cent so that the growth rate of per capita income remained negative. Among African countries, the proportion of those with less than a 3 per cent growth rate increased from 29 per cent in 1987 to 31 per cent in 1988, while those with GDP growth rates of over 3 per cent decreased from 27 per cent of all the countries in 1985 to 25 per cent in 1986 and 18 per cent by 1988. The World Bank's *World Development Report* of 1989 showed that GDP per capita in sub-Saharan Africa decreased annually by 2.5 per cent during 1980–88. Its 1990 Report on *Poverty* projects that Africa will experience the fastest growth of poverty at 43.1 per cent by the year 2000 (compared to 4.0 in East Asia, 11.4 for Latin America and a global average of 18.0) so that Africa's per capita income will fall continuously up to the next century (World Bank, 1990; p. 139). The adjustment record is so disastrous that the *Daily Times* of Nigeria reported on April 24, 1991 that the Ghanaian Head of State had openly rejected the citation of Ghana by the IMF and World Bank as a "success story" in view of the persistent stagnation of the country after 25 years of adjustment since the overthrow of President Nkrumah in 1966.

But in addition to the parlous economic indicators, there are also the catastrophic social and political impact of Fund–Bank stabilization and adjustment programmes. Even with the grafting of the Social Dimension of Adjustment (SDA) programme onto the orthodox SAPs, the social situation has continued to deteriorate as shown by the UNDP's *Human Development Report* of 1990 and similar reports by UNICEF, ILO, FAO and others. In addition to rising unemployment, starvation and malnutrition, there are falling enrolment rates at all levels of education in many countries. Thus the number of illiterates which was 124 million in 1960 rose to 162 million in 1985 and to 190 million by 1990, while 20 per cent of the world's illiterate females are in Africa. These socio-economic failures of adjustment are compounded by its negative political impact. Indeed, much of the anger of the pro-democracy riots across Africa is triggered by, and directed at, the widespread repression from the austerity measures in on-going adjustment programmes. Their built-in commitment to authoritarian regimes and the militarization of politics are most alarming here. These are additional to the systematic undermining of national sovereignty in the development of a new *colonialism* by the IMF, World Bank and their major sponsors.

Orthodox adjustment and perverse growth

Many argue that even if orthodox adjustment could achieve its professed stabilization and growth – which it has not – these would be perverse stability and perverse growth. This is because of the very nature and conceptualisation of adjustment in Africa and the rest of the Third World. In this regard, orthodox adjustment is an external imposition and the increasing subordination of Africa as the periphery of the periphery of world capitalism (Mahjoub, 1990). The real meaning of this adjustment is the *re-adjustment of African* economies to the changing requirements of global capital to deal with its deepening crisis and the growing competition of South-East Asian capital (Japan, Taiwan and other 'Asian tigers' or Newly Industrialized Countries (NICs) of that sub-region) against Western capital. *The Second Slump* of 1974–78 (Mandel, 1980) heralded this crisis of global capitalism, which arose from the rising prices of raw materials – especially oil (hence the prompt Western alliance in the recent Gulf crisis) – and the challenge from Asian capital. Hence the obsession of adjustment programmes with massive generalized devaluation to cheapen raw materials, the imposition of de-industrialization and the general trend toward new colonialism to entrench Africa as the "fourth world" – the periphery of the Third World periphery. The *net capital transfer* from the South to the North of AROUND $150 billion between 1985 and 1990 reflects the super-exploitation facilitated by this adjustment to further guarantee the expansion of global capitalism and the security of Western dominance. This on-going adjustment has been imposed by the core capitalist countries primarily to force African and other Third World regions to satisfy Western productive requirements, rather than to promote their so-called growth as alleged in the adjustment rhetoric of the IMF and

World Bank (Amin, 1974 and Fitt, 1980). Though all economies adjust continuously, orthodox adjustment programmes impose *readjustment* on Africa for the benefit of *restructuring* in the advanced capitalist countries.

Adjustment growth is also perverse as unequal growth. It reproduces the polarized and unequal development of the world capitalist system which is detrimental to Africa. It is constrained by the unacceptable requirement that Africa must pursue its imposed role of specialization in primary production within the international capitalist division of labour. This is on the basis of so-called comparative advantage – a static classical theoretical construct that is out-dated by over one hundred years. It is the theoretical basis of *unequal exchange* that generates *unequal development* of the world economy and supports the unequal growth pursued by SAPs. Thus when the IMF and World Bank impose free market prices as the core of their adjustment programmes, it must be realized that these are essentially global prices determined by the multinational corporations for the achievement of their international equilibrium of values and capital accumulation. In the world capitalist economy, African countries are simply *price-takers* – as determined by the dominant capital of the industrialized countries. So the growth which these so-called competitive prices of adjustment produce must necessarily preserve unequal growth, polarized development and the continued marginalization of Africa. Africa must reject the growth project of orthodox adjustment programmes which leads directly to a *cul de sac* – a dead end of the vicious cycle of poverty, rising global inequalities and the increasing marginalization of Africa, a process that some call "the fourth-worldization of Africa".

Moreover, this adjustment growth is a minority project – it is growth for the primary benefit of a minority or coterie of the national population. It reinforces the effects of unequal global development within each country. Some see this as the concentric circle of satellization in which the metropoles have the NICs of Asia and Latin America as their periphery (including apartheid South Africa), and Africa as the periphery of the periphery. Each Third World country also has its urban metropole and rural periphery – with exploitation and inequality intensifying from the global metropole down to the rural heartland of super-exploitation and degrading misery (Frank, 1974). Adjustment growth is thus for national minorities (representing 1 to 2 per cent of some national populations to around 10 to 20 per cent of others.

These primary adjustment beneficiaries include multinational corporations (MNCs), their senior executives and employees, top government leaders (civilian and military), technocrats, intermediary or local business community importers and exporters, currency speculators, contractors, consultants and other comprador elements that function as native collectors of the imperialist loot in various sectors under neocolonialism across Africa. The "fifth columnists" or local allies of the IMF and World Bank are among these local beneficiaries of adjustment (Payar, 1974). Whatever growth occurs under orthodox adjustment is cornered by this elite minority, and barely trickles down to the vast majority of the impoverished masses bearing the brunt of the adjustment burden. So even within countries, this adjustment growth is polarized and unequal and therefore, politically unacceptable.

Lessons of orthodox adjustment in the 1980s

To transcend the politics of adjustment, it is important to learn from the orthodox stabilization and adjustment of the 1980s (Adedeji, 1990, Ch. 9). To avoid past mistakes, we must build on our knowledge and experience of the channels of impact of major adjustment policies, their pitfalls, main beneficiaries and required modifications. This hindsight is critical to the successful re-launching of Africa's development in the 1990s. As we do not have to invent the wheel all over again, it is important to know the areas of adaptation, complementarity and substitution in the recovery process.

The important relevant lessons identified by the ECA are: (a) the need to avoid the pursuit of wrong short-term policies to the neglect of the region's long-term development objectives; (b) the role of the inherited colonial economic legacy as the root cause of Africa's persistent crisis; (c) failure of efficient resource utilization; (d) risk of marginalizing the people in the development process; (e) necessity for arresting net resource outflows from Africa; and (f) the role of poor integration in the intensification of the crisis.

On the first lesson, it is clear that orthodox adjustment programmes with their short-run concern for stabilization, narrow objectives and external pre-occupations have been foisted on African leaders to the neglect of long-term development objectives which they adopted in the Lagos Plan of Action (LPA). The desperate situation in some countries may have led some to rationalize this approach when they appealed to the IMF and World Bank for assistance. But the fact remains that the adoption of SAPs by 34 African countries has held the pursuit of their long-term development in abeyance, as the short-run policies they have been pursuing under the Fund and Bank have created additional structural problems that inhibit the achievement of these goals. Thus the pursuit of short-run balance of payments equilibrium and fiscal balance, price adjustment and similar stabilization objectives has undermined the development of human resources, food production, the satisfaction of basic needs and regional economic cooperation. The real lesson here is that African leaders must never sacrifice the pursuit of their national and collective interests for externally-imposed interests, and must develop the self-confidence to implement their own blueprints and programmes, regardless of any external advice or pressures. If African countries had resolutely pursued the implementation of their development objectives as stipulated in the LPA, the crisis of the 1980s would have been less severe, if not nipped in the bud or avoided altogether.

It is also clear that African countries cannot retain the inherited and perverse colonial economic structures and expect to avoid periodic crises, or to achieve sustainable development. The colonial economic structures have a built-in commitment to crises, stagnation and decay, economic disarticulation, lop-sided development, excessive external dependence, export vulnerability and pre-occupation with exchange activities. Africa must make a determined effort to change these perverse economic structures. The current programmes are designed to adjust African economies to the perverse requirements of unequal exchange and development, and to confine Africa to the periphery of the periphery of world capitalism. This must be reversed and African economies restructured. Diversity and strength of domestic production, advantageous patterns of production and consumption, internalization of the national and regional development, and the vigorous pursuit of regional cooperation and integration are compulsory for this reversal. Africa must rapidly achieve greater relative autonomy from world capitalism to pursue these legitimate development objectives.

The experience of the 1980s highlights the failure of efficient resource utilization. Resource waste at all levels, external leakages of resources and unproductive expenditures on white elephant projects, festivals and defence must be arrested. Across Africa, reported resource waste on costly imported equipment and other materials, new furniture in Ministries towards the end of the budget year to exhaust funds, excessive spending on administration and official travel with daily allowances over $300 and as high as $400, and an average annual defence expenditure of around $5 billion must be drastically reduced for the resolution of internal conflicts and strife. Excessive imports and the transference of domestic expenditure and investment abroad stifles the development process.

The catastrophic human costs of the crisis and adjustment in the 1980s underline the serious danger of marginalizing the people in the development process. The diverse manifestations of this include decreased popular consultation in the formulation and imposition of adjustment programmes, avoidance of popular reactions against them, massive retrenchment, heavy unemployment, grave neglect of human resource development, collapsing social services, falling enrolment, and the increasing monopoly of the benefits of adjustment by a tiny minority. Yet, the people are the most crucial factor in development and its foremost legitimate end.

An equally important lesson from the 1980s is the urgent need to arrest the increasing net outflow of resources from Africa to the North. It is perverse and scandalous that poor Africa should subsidize the opulence of the advanced capitalist countries. This graphic expression of the immorality of the external debt crisis is a reflection of the growing disparities of world capitalism in which the rich get richer and the poor become poorer. This is true both between the North and the South and within the adjusting countries. It is a moral outrage. These net resource transfers from Africa to the North were $5.8 billion in 1988 and $5.5 billion by 1989 with corresponding *net* transfers to the IMF and World Bank of $1.2 billion and $1.5 billion in the two years, respectively (Table 2.5, Chapter 2). These net transfers consist mainly of external debt service payments and capital flight. Africa has also lost enormous sums annually through the collapse of its export volumes and prices. This alarming resource drain must be stopped, and maximum resources committed to Africa's urgent recovery-with-transformation.

The final lesson of the 1980s is the absolute need for economic integration to avoid intensification of the crisis. As stated earlier, if the Lagos Plan of Action, the Monrovia Strategy and the Final Act of Lagos on the region's integration had been implemented, the current crisis would have been greatly mitigated, if not avoided altogether. The continuing fragmentation of the region's commodity and factor markets as well as production structures has contributed much to the collapse of commodity trade, balance of payments deficits, external debt, and the overall severity of the crisis. The country-by-country approach of orthodox adjustment programmes has also undermined sub-regional and regional cooperation by impeding the harmonisation of policies and ensuring enormous power over individual African countries by the Fund, Bank, Club of London and Club of Paris creditors. Hence external debt and SAP negotiations are invariably tilted against the atomized African countries.

Two ideological and political lessons arise from the experiences of the 1980s. One concerns the growing severity of the constraints imposed by world capitalism on Africa's development. This is commonly called the increasing hostility of the international economic environment, which is reflected in the viciousness and immorality of the external debt crisis, the stringent and pernicious demands of orthodox adjustment and the protracted deterioration of Africa's commodity trade. While these reflect the growing intensity of the crisis of world capitalism and its subsequent need for increasing exploitation of the periphery, they also demonstrate the extreme difficulty of African countries in achieving sustainable development on the basis of current adjustment rules. The very motive for these rules is the maintenance of the *status quo* with the growing marginalization of Africa. This is the pertinent meaning of the need to transcend the politics of adjustment, to transcend the rules of the game, to arrest unequal exchange, unequal growth and polarized development. This is the agenda that confronts Africa in the 1990s and beyond.

The political lesson from the 1980s involves the correct understanding of the true nature of the current crisis. As stated in Chapter 3, the external debt crisis is a Financial Low Intensity Conflict (FLIC), an undeclared economic war of recolonization. Orthodox stabilization and SAPs with their tough conditionalities are weapons in this war. Understanding of this *political strategy* in the crisis is a fundamental pre-condition for its resolution. The IMF, World Bank and their supporters falsely present the crisis as an economistic problem of efficiency and demand management. While there *are* economic questions and efficiency issues involved, the external debt crisis and the net transfer of around $50 billion annually from the South to the North is not inevitable. Is the spread of the use of conditionality from the IMF to the World Bank, to bilateral donors, to Lomé IV, ESAF, International Commodity Fund and other areas inevitable? Is the practice of the World Bank in always preparing a counter-programme to Africa's collective blueprints (e.g. its Berg Report Vs. Africa's LPA, Long-term Perspective Study, LTPS, Vs. Africa's Alternative Framework, etc.) a purely economic accident, or the implementation of a political strategy to subordinate Africa's interests? Is it purely on economic grounds that the $14 billion OECD Bank for the Reconstruction and Development of Eastern Europe under Attari has taken off within one year in London while Africa is left in the lurch? It is for these reasons that African leaders must recognize the strong political factor in the current crisis, and take concerted and collective *political action* to deal effectively with it. This demands the revamping of the OAU, urgent formation of an *African debtors' cartel,* linked to Latin American and Asian debtors' cartels to counter the creditors' cartels. It requires the urgent *political will* to pursue African cooperation and integration vigorously from the 1990s.

Building on existing consensus

Happily, consensus is emerging on many of these issues among the major parties involved, especially between African countries and their international development partners, and between the ECA and the Bretton Woods institutions as detailed by the World Bank in its *Long-term Perspective Study,* LTPS (World Bank, 1989). Four things are important about this consensus, namely: (a) ensuring that it is not just used as a propaganda stunt; (b) careful identification of the areas of agreement; (c) urgent implementation of the existing consensus; and (d) expansion of consensus through official dialogue to the remaining areas of disagreement.

On the first issue, it is unfortunate that the World Bank has used emerging consensus as a propaganda gimmick to avert further criticism. It has readily announced its agreement with the ECA, which is generally welcome. But this should not be an issue for scoring debating points. For Africa, this consensus is important for transcending the adjustment debate to the stage of positive and cooperative *action*. Emergent consensus should not be reduced to rhetoric for diverting public attention and averting criticisms of the failure of on-going SAPs and the persistence of the crisis.

The areas of agreement must be identified to focus attention on the areas where cooperative action is feasible and where further dialogue is needed. In the famous *Joint Statement* of May 1989 between the ECA, OAU, ADB (African Development Bank) and World Bank, the areas of agreement were indicated as follows:

> The future challenge is to assist Africa to transform the condition of its economies still threatened with stagnation and decline to sustainable growth with equity. While sustainable economic growth is imperative, it is only the means to the overarching objectives of improving human welfare – for example, reducing infant mortality, increasing educational opportunity, improving health and ensuring food security. Economic adjustment must lead to the long-term improvement in the quality of life of the African peoples. Particular attention should be given to protecting vulnerable groups during the adjustment process, including protection of core budget expenditures on social sector programmes. Special emphasis should be placed on employment opportunities. The shortage of technical skills and weak institutions are major impediments to Africa's growth and development. Priority should be given, therefore, to human resource development and national capacity building.

The World Bank emphasizes these areas of consensus in the LTPS (World Bank, 1989, pp. 14–15 and 183) as the need for adjustment with sustainable growth and equity, fundamental transformation of Africa's production structures, people-centred and human resource development, capacity building, enabling policy environment, food security through agricultural research and extension services, regional integration and popular participation.

What is still lacking is the urgent implementation of these areas of agreement. The World Bank states that orthodox adjustment is still evolving and "new generation SAPs" are to be expected. But when will the areas of agreement be translated into concrete policy actions? In the *Joint Statement* cited above, this concern with action was also raised:

> as the basic approach to adjustment issues has evolved, it has become clear that adjustment must be seen as part of a long-term development approach and that it must take full account of the human dimension. *Stronger efforts are required to assure that this consensus is translated into action*

(author's emphasis). This is precisely the problem – when will this consensus be implemented through the appropriate change of on-going SAPs?

Grafting the social dimension of adjustment (SDA) onto orthodox SAPs is useless. Adjustment programmes have to be re-designed to incorporate these areas of consensus in a holistic manner – not through piecemeal grafting of bits and pieces onto already failed, orthodox SAPs. This is also why the *African Capacity Building Initiative,* ACBI (World Bank, 1990) co-sponsored by the World Bank, UNDP and ADB is welcome but inadequate – it is another graft onto failed SAPs. As long as the current SAPs remain in force, Africa's capacity problem will persist. Thus as long as the massive currency devaluation and high external debt service continue, so long will the massive brain drain from African countries persist – in spite of ACBI. Massive retrenchment, subsidy withdrawal across-the-board, drastic budget and credit squeeze, high interest rates, doctrinaire privatization and net resource transfers to the IMF and World Bank are also major sources of the weakening of Africa's capacity in education, health and other social services, manpower development and utilization, research and development. The on-going SAPs have to be replaced by more relevant alternative programmes that incorporate capacity requirements in production, technology, distribution, popular participation and new power relations in a holistic and systematic manner, rather than grafting them on in a piecemeal and distorted fashion.

It is equally necessary to continue dialogue between Africa, on one hand, and the Bretton Woods institutions and foreign development partners, on the other, on the areas of disagreement. The important issues of dialogue are the appropriate roles of planning and free market prices, especially for exchange rate policy; the optimal balance between the public and private sectors; industrialization strategy, particularly for industries in the intermediate and capital-goods areas; the necessity for delinking, structural disengagement of "selective closure" against the total liberalization of imports and African economies; and the issue of regional food self-sufficiency demanded by Africa and the food security planned in orthodox adjustment programmes. What should be primary in this dialogue is Africa's legitimate need for accelerated recovery-with-transformation. Once this is accepted, the accumulated empirical experience with on-going SAPs since the 1980s should give adequate guidance on these outstanding issues. Hence the need to review the evidence of the negative impact of each of these disputed policies to decide from the circumstances of individual countries on the best course of action. The Bretton Woods institutions must be less doctrinaire in their pursuit of liberal capitalism to introduce necessary flexibility into the design and implementation of adjustment-with-transformation.

Adjustment, transformation and delinking

The issues surrounding adjustment, transformation and delinking have featured in the adjustment debate since the 1980s and, as we move Africa's agenda forward, it should be fairly clear what the consensus and continuing disagreement are on these issues, and what the policy options indicate.

Adjustment and transformation

In this regard, there is happily some consensus on the questions of *adjustment and transformation,* on one hand, and transformation and delinking, on the other. The implied relationship between adjustment and delinking, however, is still sharply contested. Thus it is generally agreed that Africa must go beyond endless and narrow adjustment to simultaneously embark on structural transformation, the rhetoric of the Bretton Woods institutions remains "adjustment and growth with equity". Africa demands and is poised for adjustment-with-transformation to eliminate the structural bottlenecks that constitute the root causes of the crisis. Human resource development and capacity building, to which the Bretton Woods institutions are so positively inclined, imply transformation and not mere growth, which has occurred without much development or transformation of the African economies since the 1960s.

Transformation and delinking

Although the linkage between these issues is clear in the literature, they are less frequently discussed in policy circles. (Amin, 1990 and Mahjoub, 1990). Their common grounds include the reduction of external dependence (by the African periphery on the advanced capitalist or centre countries), the emphasis on popular participation and empowerment of the people, democratization of the benefits of development, elimination of the extreme disarticulation of the peripheral economies and increased relative autonomy for the African economies. Beyond these, however, two important areas of non-convergence between transformation and delinking remain, including the conceptualization of the global context and the ideological requirement for delinking. Thus from the Lagos Plan of Action (LPA) to AAF–SAP, official discussion of transformation does not adequately analyse Africa's development in terms of the dialectics of world capitalism, the logic of the capitalist international division of labour between the centre and peripheral counties, unequal exchange and unequal global development. This may be due largely to the diplomatic etiquette that informs ECA, OAU and ADB discourse, and to their need to build consensus with the North. As a result their realization and acceptance of the political implications and socio-economic constraints on Africa's drive for transformation is questionable.

The difference between the transformers and the delinkists is more overtly ideological with respect to their strategies for Africa's transformation and understanding of the social forces or class configuration of the political programme for Africa's transformation. These issues are usually avoided in Africa's official discourse – though the Bretton Woods institutions are frenetic and open about their doctrinaire commitment to liberal capitalism. Delinking argues for a truly democratic socialist transition implemented by the majority who are maginalized by on-going orthodox adjustment, including workers, peasants, women, youths, students and patriotic professionals and politicians. These social forces are also implied by the bearers of popular participation, but instead of the democratic socialist transition, the World Bank recommends the Social Market Economy of the Nordic countries for Africa (World Bank, 1989, p. 187). But African transformers veer towards a Pragmatic Mixed Economy.

Clearly there is need for an ideological dialogue between the transformers, the delinkists and the Bretton Woods institutions – a dialogue which many may see as a chat between the deaf and the dumb.

Adjustment and delinking

The gulf between orthodox adjustment and delinking is the widest among the three strategies identified here, i.e. adjustment, transformation and delinking. This is hardly surprising as delinking has not been officially endorsed as an African collective position, and features little in the official adjustment debate. Its strong advocates are mostly critical social scientists and other progressive social forces, including politicians in some countries, but these are not central negotiators for Africa. The major disagreements between adjustment and delinking centre on the perverse nature of adjustment growth discussed above. It is that basically, adjustment is an exploitative demand on African economies to meet the reproductive requirements of the advanced capitalist countries, so that it subordinates Africa's legitimate development needs to the dictates of unequal growth, polarized development and the unequal exchange of world capitalism. So unless Africa delinks or disengages relatively from this exploitative strait-jacket, it has little prospect of transformation or of achieving its long-term development objectives.

But the real disagreement between adjustment and delinking lies in the choice of ideology, or the path to Africa's development. While the proponents of adjustment in the Bretton Woods institutions and outside them prescribe liberal capitalism or at best the Nordic social market economy, the delinkists call for a genuinely democratic socialist transition based on effective popular participation. Their political programme is a broad democratic alliance of popular social forces for the pursuit of people-centred development, through the empowerment of the people and the democratization of power and distribution.

They admit that this is a difficult transition that has been attempted by radical to conservative regimes under African or Arab socialism in the past. The reforms in Eastern Europe have seen the reversal of these delinking experiments – a reversal propelled by the ideological attack of orthodox adjustment and its market theology. But since the marginalization of Africa as the periphery of the periphery has persisted and the orthodox SAPs have failed disastrously, many feel that some form of delinking, structural disengagement from world capitalism or selective closure must be part of the agenda for transcending the politics of adjustment from the 1990s. This seems to explain many of the common grounds between transformation and delinking – expressed as national and collective self-reliance, internalization of the engine of Africa's development and the inward-looking strategy.

Africa's agenda for the 1990s and beyond.

African countries and the Bretton Woods institutions have each produced blueprints for Africa's socio-economic agenda in the 1990s. On the part of Africa, this collective regional agenda for transcending the politics of adjustment consists of the following blueprints:

- Lagos Plan of Action (LPA), the Monrovia Strategy and the Final Act of Lagos for Africa's Economic Development from 1980 to year 2000 (by the OAU);
- *ECA's Revised Perspective for Africa's Development* from 1990 to year 2008[1];
- African Alternative Framework (AAF–SAP) in Chapter 5 and its Selected Policy Instruments (forthcoming);
- Africa's Common Position on External Debt (OAU, December 1987) and revised for the Conference on Africa's Least Developed Countries, LDCs, in Paris in September 1990;
- Africa's Common Position on the Frazer Report titled *Africa's Commodity Problems – Towards a Solution* (OAU, 1990);
- Draft Treaty Establishing the African Economic Community (OAU) – to be ratified by the OAU Summit at Abuja, Nigeria, in June 1991;
- African charter for Popular Participation in Development, ACPPD (ECA) – discussed in Chapter 6.

These deal with the major problems that have been identified as priorities for African countries in the 1990s (Adedeji, 1990, Chs. 8 and 9). These are: external debt and debt servicing; food and population; commodity trade; environmental degradation; socio-economic cooperation and integration; peace and full democratization with popular participation.

Correspondingly, Africa's foreign development partners and members of the UN system have also produced blueprints for Africa's development in the 1990s:

1. This ECA long-term perspective study for Africa's development was first published in 1987, for 1980 to year 2000 but revised in 1988–89 for 1990 to year 2008.

- *World Bank:*
  Poverty – World Development Report, 1990; *Long-term Perspective Study* (LTPS) with Chapter 9 titled "A Strategic Agenda (for Sub-Saharan Africa) for the 1990s"; *African Capacity Building Initiative* (ACBI) with UNDP and ADB.
- *UNDP:*
  Human Development Report 1990 – a first annual report; ACBI with the World Bank and ADB.
- *FAO:*
  Projected Estimate of Africa's Food Situation to year 2000.
- *UN General Assembly:*
  Frazer Report on *Africa's Commodity Problems – Towards a Solution* – prepared for the Secretary-General of the UN.

These major socio-economic problems confronting Africa in the 1990s and the blueprints on them can be classified as shown in Table 7.1.

Table 7.1 African and foreign perspectives on the resolution of the African crisis

	Blueprints for the 1990s				
Main Problems	Africa's	World Bank	UNDP	FAO	UN
1. External Debts	4	None	–	–	–
2. Food and Population	2, 3	Poverty Report	Human Dev. Report	Food Estimate	–
3. Commodity trade	1, 2, 5, 6	LTPS, Ch. 9	–	–	Frazer Report
4. Environmental Degradation	UNCED-1992	LTPS, Ch. 9	–	–	–
5. Regional Integration	1, 2, 6	LTPS, Ch. 9	–	–	–
6. Democratisation	7	LTPS, Ch. 9	None	None	None

Note: Numbers under Africa's refer to the listing of Africa's 7 blueprints under Section 7.5 above.

Table 7.1 summarizes consensus and divergence on how to resolve the African crisis beyond the adjustment debate. Thus the World Bank has no strategic agenda for dealing with external debt and debt servicing in the 1990s, while its Capacity Building Initiative (ACBI) does not focus directly on any one of Africa's six priority problems – though it touches all of them peripherally. The Bank's perspectives in its "strategic agenda for the 1990s" (Ch. 9 of LTPS) reflect differences between African and Western perspectives, as summarized below:

> There is a striking contrast between African and Western Perspectives . . . The African viewpoint, particularly that of politicians, must assume a future that is economically viable and politically sustainable. It must assume industrialization and, at least a promise of technological equality with the West (including Japan). It must encompass spiritual health and self-reliance as well as material well-being. The perspective is quite naturally Afro-centric.
>
> . . . The Western perspective is that of the policy-maker . . . Africa does not dominate this perspective, it is only one of a panoply of global concerns. Unlike the African politician, the Western bureaucrat is not compelled to assume politically viable solutions within Africa, nor does he take for granted the feasibility of rapid economic progress. Quite the contrary, he is usually more impressed by the negative, short-term implications of Africa's economic crisis – particularly its effect on political stability . . .

"These differing perspectives, African and Western, are reflected in two much-discussed documents, the 'Lagos Plan of Action' and the report of the World Bank entitled 'Accelerated Development in Sub-Saharan Africa: an Agenda for Action' [i.e. Berg Report]", says A. Adedeji in *The African Alternative,* (p. 54). Besides disagreement on the Lagos Plan of Action there are other differences on the perceptions of the region's major problems and their solutions.

Africa's perception of its priority problems

Africa's perception of its priority problems and their solutions is fully articulated in the relevant blueprints that the region has prepared and adopted collectively on each of the major problems as indicated in Table 7.1.

Foreign debt and reparations payment

Africa's Common Position in External Debt calls for the solutions indicated in Chapter 3. Collectively, the external debt relief measures required include the termination of the slightly over $1 billion in annual net transfer to the IMF and World Bank; the elimination of the over $20 billion of total debt service payments due from Africa annually, with about $10 billion of that due to rising interest rates on these immoral debts; the cancellation of the total foreign debt of around $46 billion owed by Africa's 29 least developed countries

(LDCs); and the cancellation or collective repudiation of the remaining external debt.[2] As argued in Chapter 3, these bogus debts have been repaid in many respects.

Africa, like the Afro-Americans, is also demanding reparations payments from world capitalism, especially from Western Europe and the USA, for eight centuries of slavery, 100 years of colonization and three decades of neo-colonial depredations, exploitation and wanton plunder. This was the subject of an *International Conference on Reparations Payment* – to Africa and Peoples of African Descent in the Diaspora – which was held in Lagos in December 1990. The Conference established an International Committee to document the case to be submitted to the OAU Summit in Abuja, Nigeria, in June 1991. The evidence rests on German reparations payment for war damages during World War I, the estimated $718 billion[3] so far paid by Germany for the death of 2 million Jews during World War II, and the Japanese receipt of reparations payments from the USA since World War II. Hence Africa's entitlements for the losses of an estimated 30 million people during the slave trade, several millions of lives in colonial wars and billions of dollars in physical destruction and plunder during slavery, colonialism and neo-colonialism cannot be disputed. Some raise the question of capacity for enforcement as the determinant factor in past reparations payment and point to Africa's relative weakness in the world community. But this is secondary to the real issue as to whether on historical, legal, political, economic and moral grounds, Africa can, and should, make a claim for reparations payment. The world economy and international capitalism must know that Africa is a *net creditor* to them, and not to be pilloried for immoral debts. The reparations payment owed to Africa runs into trillions of dollars and is more than enough to offset Africa's alleged external debt.

Food and population

The problems of pervasive starvation or physical hunger and malnutrition underscore Africa's current and projected food deficit. The FAO has estimated food import requirements of 8.2 million tons of which only 3.8 million tons were to be covered by food aid by 1989. Even by year 2000, it is projected that the food self-sufficiency ratios which stood at 74.1 per cent for cereals during 1980–87 would have

2. The cancellation or collective repudiation of external debt is not part of the OAU Common Position on these debts, but it is the position of IFAA, OATUU and many other mass organizations in Africa.

3. This figure was presented and used during the Reparations Conference.

risen only to 90.0 per cent (with 100 per cent for other food items by then). Hence the demand that 20–25 per cent of total public investment should be devoted to agriculture, especially the food sub-sector. This is to correct the embarrassing anomaly by which Africa is the only region in the world yet to generate an Agrarian Revolution – whose raw materials should propel a parallel Industrial Revolution through agro-allied industries. Price support policy for food production, selective subsidies, discriminatory credit control in favour of agriculture, differential interest rates that favour food production and multiple exchange rates that offer incentives to agricultural production are also included in Africa's blueprints on food and agriculture (these are AAF–SAP, its Selected Policy Instruments and the ECA's Revised Perspective on Africa's Development). Though the World Bank's *Poverty* Report and LTPS also deal with the food problem, they emphasize food security through unreliable food aid and food import, instead of food self-sufficiency through domestic food production.

Rapid population growth rate at an average of 3 per cent – the highest in the world, together with spatial maldistribution of the population also poses a serious demographic problem for the region. In addition to the blueprints mentioned for food, Africa has also been implementing the *Kilimanjaro Plan of Action* on population control (ECA, 1989). The *Khartoum Declaration* (ECA, 1988) on human resource development has also been adopted, and these are complemented by the UNDP's *Human Development Report* of 1990 and the World Bank's LTPS concern with the demographic problem. All these emphasize the need for an active population policy in each country, family planning, spatial redistribution of population through regional planning and land reforms to ease rural landlessness as well as the promotion of labour-intensive methods of production to facilitate labour absorption.

Africa's commodity trade

This is being addressed through the revamping of the LPA, ECA's Revised Perspective, Africa's Common Position on the Frazer Report and the Draft Treaty of the African Economic Community. Improved export trade and better external debt relief hold the key to the financing of Africa's adjustment-with-transformation. Thus ECA has calculated that low commodity prices have cost Africa \$54.3 billion in lost export earnings during 1981–87 with a loss of \$19 billion in one year during 1985–86. These exclude the effect of falling export volume due to protectionist measures against the region's commodity export and synthetic substitution for its raw materials. Lomé IV has offered little respite from this collapse of commodity trade, while the Uruguay Round of GATT negotiations for liberalizing world trade have been estimated to impose a *net loss* of around $3 billion annually on African countries (Bhagavan, 1989 and Knudsen et al. 1989). Though the World Bank attributes the collapse of Africa's commodity trade to declining international competitiveness, the main causes are the collapse of International Commodity Agreements in the 1980s, protectionist measures against Africa's exports, and deteriorating terms of trade, caused partly by massive and persistent devaluation imposed by the IMF and World Bank. Thus Africa's 25 coffee producing countries were estimated to lose $150 million in 1990 alone from the collapse of the International Coffee Agreement.

The Single European Market of 1992 is likely to worsen Africa's exports by removing many concessions made to Africa under the Lomé Convention. The associated deterioration in Africa's terms of trade is show in Chapter 2, Table 2.3.

The International Commodity Fund – offered as a solution to this export problem – is too small relative to the magnitude of the problem, and drawing from it is difficult because of its conditionalities. Progress with STABEX and SYSMIN for the stabilization of export and import prices has been slow. Frazer's Report on *Africa's Commodity Problems* in 1990 that was commissioned by the UN Secretary-General was so bad that two members of the Committee refused to sign it (i.e. the representatives of France and Nigeria). The OAU also rejected the Report because of its conservatism and recommendation as its main solution the promotion of the same old traditional exports that led to the region's trade problem. The Report is a rehash of World Bank views on Africa's exports. The OAU's *Common Position* on the Report (OAU, 1990) calls for vigorous export diversification, the processing of raw materials before export, the restoration of International Commodity Agreements, enlarged international compensatory financing for export losses, the lifting of protectionist barriers against exports of primary products and manufactured goods from Africa.

Environmental degradation

This is a major problem involving desertification, drought, deforestation and soil erosion. Desertification at an estimated annual rate of 70 kilometers is the most serious as Africa has the world's largest desert mass in the Sahara and Kalahari. The drought of 1973–75 and 1983–85 in the Sahel which led to the loss of about one-third of the GDP of the Sahel countries is also a major ecological hazard. These have been compounded by massive deforestation and soil erosion caused largely by excessive cultivation and over-grazing to increase exports and pay foreign debts. Environmental pollution, "greenhouse effect" or global warming, micro-climate change, insect invasion (locusts and grasshoppers) and wildlife depletion have also been increasing at alarming rates. Africa has prepared the *Kampala Agenda for Action* of 1990 as a summary of earlier environmental initiatives for dealing with these problems. The region is also preparing hard for the UN Conference on Environment and Development (UNCED) billed for Brazil in 1992. It is to provide a coordinated global opportunity to find effective and durable solutions to these environmental problems that are more severe in Africa than in any other region of the world – largely because of the extreme poverty and underdevelopment of the region, which exacerbate environmental degradation.

Regional cooperation and integration

This issue is addressed by three African blueprints – the Lagos Plan of Action (LPA), (with revamping planned for its Tenth Anniversary Conference in Lagos in December 1990), the ECA Revised Perspective and the Draft Treaty of the African Economic Community. Integration has been rightly identified as the central strategy for the structural transformation of African economies. This is dictated by the extreme fragmentation of factor and product markets as well as production structures, and the non-viability of most national economies in the region that are based on mini-states each with a population of less than 10 million (Nyongo, 1990). The prospects of Europe 1992 and growing economic regionalism in North America around the USA and in the Pacific Rim around Japan and Taiwan also pose a direct threat and challenge for Africa's accelerated integration. The illusion of independent national development has been shattered by the crisis of the 1980s and must be jettisoned. So the political will to defeat foreign machinations against the region's integration, especially by France, must be urgently mustered. The World Bank should also support, in addition to *market integration, production integration* in its LTPS, to internalise the region's engine of development as planned in Africa's blueprints. All these require full support for the energetic and rapid establishment of the African Economic Community whose current time-table is excessively conservative and must be drastically shortened to establish the Community by year 2000 or soon thereafter. Effective funding should derive from indirect taxation (e.g. about 2 per cent addition to national import and excise taxes to be levied and paid for sub-regional and regional integration, (including the effective funding of the OAU), rather than reliance on member-state contributions, strengthening of existing sub-regional groupings like ECOWAS, PTA, SADCC, ECCAS and Magreb Union and enlisting the popular participation of trade unions, Chambers of Commerce, women and peasant organizations, students' unions and professional associations in the integration process. This sub-regional and regional cooperation for national and collective self-reliance should also promote South-South Cooperation (South Commission, 1990).

Peace and democratization

Internal conflicts and strife, political instability and pervasive lack of democracy are also critical problems that must be resolved as Africa transcends the adjustment debate of the 1980s. The OAU is revamping its Commission on Conflict Resolution and paying closer attention to the spate of internal conflicts that threatens the peace, security and stability which are so crucial for development, dissipate limited development resources and create horrendous refugee problems. As the denial of democratic rights and political participation are important causes of these domestic conflicts, the African Charter for Popular Participation has directly addressed these problems. The control of foreign interventions in Africa and the termination of the support of Western governments for fascist , dictatorial and oppressive regimes in African countries are also critical here. In order to be a decade of adjustment with transformation, the 1990s must also be a decade for peace and full democratization across Africa.

Two approaches to resolving Africa's problems

For launching Africa's recovery-with-transformation in the 1990s, two approaches, the *historical and normative* trends or scenarios are contrasted by the ECA in its *Long-term Perspective on Africa's Development* (ECA 1983 and 1988). The historical approach reaches a "nightmare scenario" that is rejected, while the normative trend generates Africa's desired state by year 2000.

The historical trends scenario

If African countries were to persist in their implementation of orthodox SAPs in the 1990s, with the traditional emphasis on demand management and drastic reductions in domestic expenditures, the overall macro-economic framework shows that GDP growth rates would fall, as would per capita incomes. Even if the growth in GDP were maintained at the current level of 1.5 per cent as we enter into the 1990s, a decline would have set in by 1992, with GDP rising by only 0.9 per cent annually during 1993–96 and 0.7 per cent between 1997 and 2000. With a projected population growth rate of at least 3 per cent, income per head would further decline in the 1990s, from –1.7 per cent in 1990–1992 to –2.4 per cent in 1993–1996 and –2.2 per cent in 1997–2000. Expenditure on GDP would similarly decline, with private consumption growing by no more than the rate of 0.9 per cent that prevailed during the 1983–85 Great African Drought, while public expenditure would at best grow by a mere 3 per cent compared to the 4 per cent growth rate recorded in the 1980s (Adedeji, 1990, p.102).

With emphasis on demand management, high interest rates and credit squeeze in the historical approach, the savings-investment gap would rise as the savings ratio would fall significantly further by the end of the 1990s due to the projected fall in incomes. There is thus a very strong possibility of the resource gap rising from 13.9 per cent at the beginning of the 1990s to 15.2 per cent at the end of the decade. Food production and agriculture would grow by no more than 0.7 per cent annually in the 1990s, while the food security level will fall each year by –2.4 per cent, particularly for cereals, meat and pulses. Industrial production will also be reduced by total price and import liberalization and total credit squeeze in orthodox SAPs. Industrial growth would hardly exceed 2.7 per cent annually because of the sector's heavy dependence on imported raw materials, spare parts, equipment and skilled manpower. Capacity utilization would decline further and many more enterprises would close down. Generalized and massive devaluation would also escalate excessive inflation and price spirals, increase capital flight, divert scarce foreign exchange to speculative activities and worsen income inequalities.

Under this scenario, the value of exports is most likely to stagnate in the 1990s at their 1980–87 average level. Concentration on traditional exports would also lead to export earnings falling in real terms from \$59.2 billion during 1980–87 to \$58.9 billion by year 2000. Merchandise imports would grow annually by 4 per cent from \$74.7 billion in 1990–92 to \$81.8 billion in 1993–96 and \$90.3 billion by 1997–2000. Hence the balance of payments position would worsen as the trade deficit (imports minus exports) increases. Correspondingly, the conditions and modalities of external aid and resource flows to Africa would worsen. From projections, at best Africa may receive \$21.9 billion annually in the 1990s, while the trade gap (imports minus exports) would be \$31.4 billion annually apart from the domestic resource gaps (see Table 7.2). The level of external resource inflow would, therefore, be inadequate to finance Africa's recovery-and-transformation in the 1990s. Hence the necessity for an alternative scenario with different strategies of adjustment-with-transformation.

The normative trends scenario

The catastrophic implications of the historical approach make it imperative for African countries to discard the orthodox historical path and adopt an alternative normative development path with determination and full vigour. This normative approach is centred on the design and implementation of alternative recovery-with-transformation programmes in conformity with the African Alternative Framework to Structural Adjustment Programmes for Socio-Economic Recovery and Transformation (AAF-SAP).

Table 7.2: External resource flows to Africa, 1980–88 ($ billion)

	1980	1986	1987	1988
Official Development Finance (ODF)	10.6	15.4	18.1	20.4
Official Development Assistance (ODA)	8.9	13.4	15.1	14.7
Bilateral	6.4	9.4	10.7	–
Multilateral	2.5	4.0	4.4	–
Other ODF	1.8	2.0	3.0	5.7
Export credits	1.8	–0.1	–0.2	0.6
Private flows	3.7	4.2	4.0	4.2
Total external flows	16.1	19.5	21.9	25.2
Total flows at 1987 prices and exchange rates	21.3	22.4	21.9	23.5

Source: ECA, Economic Report on Africa 1990, (Addis Ababa), p. 31.

Under the normative trend scenario, the average annual growth rate of GDP would rise substantially in the 1990s to between 5.3 and 5.9 per cent. Both the savings and investment ratios would also increase significantly from higher incomes and lower interest rates, considerably diminishing the savings gap. The savings ratio will rise to 25.2 per cent by year 2000 compared to 17 per cent under the historical trend. The saving-investment gap will, therefore, narrow from 14.2 per cent of GDP under the historical trend to a manageable 8 per cent.

The allocation of 20–25 per cent of total public investment to agriculture, together with land reforms and improved access to agricultural inputs, would also initiate sector transformation and greatly increase food production. Agricultural and food production would grow by 4 to 5 per cent annually between 1993 and 2000, with food security levels turning positive from 1993, rising to 2.1 per cent between 1987 and 2000. Food self-sufficiency ratios for staple food crops will rise to 100 per cent by 2000 – except for cereals which would increase from 74.1 to 90 per cent by year 2000. Correspondingly, Africa will launch its industrial take-off by the year 2000 as industrial production would grow in the 1990s by 6 to 8 per cent along the normative trend compared to about 3 per cent on the historical path. The devotion of an average of 30 per cent of annual government spending to the social service sector would also ensure the revival of education, health and related social services facing imminent collapse on the historical trend.

In the external sector, the balance of payments will improve significantly under the normative approach. Vigorous diversification and processing of exports and pressure for privileged concessionary access to foreign markets for Africa's exports, including semi-manufactured and fully manufactured products will achieve this end. The drastic reduction of non-essential imports and those with local substitutes will also be essential.

Required policy shifts at national, regional and international levels

The successful achievement of Africa's "willed future" in the normative trends scenario requires the pursuit of vigorous policy shifts based on an alternative conceptualization of the African crisis and the strategies for its resolution. This involves joint responsibilities at national, regional and international levels.

Changes in conceptualization of the crisis

The correct perception and understanding of a problem is central to its solution. This applies perfectly to the protracted crisis in Africa and it requires critical review and alternative conceptualization in Africa and at the international level.

Africa

At both national and regional levels in Africa, it is important to situate the African problem in its correct global context of a world in transition and the dynamics of international capitalism. This is realism, not ideology, at least in the narrow sense. What is happening in Africa must be analysed and understood in the context of the *motives* of the dominant capital, the major industrialized countries and the Bretton Woods institutions. It must be seen in the context of the increasing challenge of South-East Asia to Western Europe and North America, growing regional economic blocs and the unfolding World Democratic Revolution. These impose three alternative perceptions of the crisis in Africa.

(a) *Political nature of crisis* – This crisis is not just a narrow economistic crisis as the IMF and World Bank want us to believe, but also a fundamentally political question. Given the Financial Low Intensity Conflict (FLIC) in the external debt crisis, Africa must see this crisis basically as political – it is the implementation of a *political strategy of subordination, recolonization and new colonialism.* Its objective is super-exploitation – to subordinate Africa further to ensure easy access to its resources and markets (including its brain power) for dealing with the problems of capital accumulation in world capitalism and the challenge from Asia. This is primarily why there must be conditionality on a scale that is absolutely unprecedented in the entire history of the world – it is why there must be an unnecessary and immoral foreign debt crisis with the hiking of interest rates to extort billions of dollars from poor Africa and the rest of the Third World. This is why the creditor countries must be cartelized into the Club of London and Club of Paris and deal with debtor countries one by one to exert maximum power over them and extort maximum resources from them. This is also why conditionality must spread to almost all international transactions – capital flows, Lomé IV, International Commodity Fund, etc. This explains why the IMF and World Bank have suddenly become imperial overseers and supra-national dictators on behalf of the erstwhile colonial powers and credit countries. It is partly why Africa's commodity trade collapsed and International Commodity Agreements were scrapped or suspended. Unless and until this political character of the crisis – and the political nature of orthodox SAPs – is fully understood in Africa, not much progress will be made in resolving it. After all, Ghana has been adjusting for 25 years now without any end in sight. These do not deny important economic issues in the crisis – Africa's contribution to them and ultimate responsibility for their resolution. Moreover, unless African countries get their internal politics right, recovery and transformation will be very difficult.

(b) *Necessity for concerted political action* – The concerted nature of the crisis demands concerted and collective political action by African countries. Rather than passing benign resolutions as in the past, this means collective decision-making, commitment and determination regardless of the opposition, and vigorous implementation. This is when Africa will be taken seriously by the rest of the world – it is only then that Africa can expect a fair deal and respect from the rest of the world. *It will be impossible to resolve the external debt crisis unless African countries take and implement collective decisions on the issue,* rather than making futile individual efforts to honour their so-called foreign debts. It is the path of folly. African countries must also act decisively together with determination on the other major regional problems – rejection of orthodox SAPs, implementation of the African Alternative Framework (AAF-SAP), commodity trade, etc. on which happily they have already adopted collective positions. This is the political way forward for Africa.

(c) *Concurrent recovery with transformation* – The correct appreciation of the current crisis as a long-term structural problem of lack of productive capacity and unequal development is also central. This is to say that the economic dimensions of the crisis are largely structural, though their manifestations may take the form of financial imbalances – balance of payments deficits, budget deficits, etc. These financial problems must be tackled alongside the structural bottlenecks. Hence the need for recovery-with-transformation. Africa must reject the plan to adjust or stabilize first before resuming its growth and transformation. Without attacking the structural causes of the problem, there can be little prospect of resolving the financial problems. This is why the on-going orthodox SAPs should be rejected in favour of the African Alternative, which incorporates the simultaneous pursuit of recovery and transformation.

International level

There is parallel need for reconceptualization of the crisis and its resolution at the international level in the following areas:

(a) *Problem perception* – The international and Western perspective of the African crisis requires important changes. The current perception is that the problem is chronic (hence the talk of aid fatigue); it is one of short-run financial imbalances amenable to the quick-fix solution of one to two-year stabilization and adjustment programmes; and it has been caused primarily by Africa's inefficiency. The problem is long-term and structural but not chronic because the African economy showed impressive growth and some transformation in the 1960s and 1970s when the international environment was more favourable as World Bank and other reports show. Africa's problem is also unlike that of the industrialized countries with periodic insufficient demand or crisis of under-consumption, and is rather a problem of low productive capacity and supply shortages. Hence the solution cannot be demand management – it is supply creation and capacity expansion through production, technology, human resource development, etc. These are long-term goals, change from the production of coffee or cocoa to the processing of raw materials, for instance, takes five to ten years.

(b) *Adjustment by deficit and surplus countries* – The need for adjustment to disequilibrium in the theoretical sense requires both the deficit and surplus countries to adjust concurrently. This is to make it possible for the deficit or debtor countries to export more and earn increased foreign exchange for the diversification and expansion of their economies. But what has happened in the current crisis is that the surplus creditor countries have imposed protectionist measures, reduced capital flows to the deficit/debtor countries while extracting net outflows from them. These measures make the recovery of the deficit/debtor countries very difficult, if not impossible. This perversion of even and balanced expansion of the world economy has instituted the current unequal growth and polarised development. Africa must not be a shunted coach of the moving locomotive of world economy – at least because this planet belongs to us all.

(c) *Western responsibility to Africa* – The point must be underlined that Western countries have a clear economic and moral responsibility to African countries in this crisis. Centuries of super-exploitation of Africa's human and physical resources from slave trade, colonialism and contemporary neocolonialism, the perverse structures imposed by colonialism and the corrupt, repressive puppet regimes installed and maintained by Western countries, are all central to the generation and entrenchment of Africa's crisis. So if the Western countries (OECD) can initiate a $14 billion Bank for Reconstruction and Development for Eastern Europe, they have an even more urgent moral responsibility to provide funds for the support of Africa's accelerated recovery and transformation. This is a demand for *justice,* not passing the buck or denying Africa's responsibility for its future.

Policy shifts in Africa and the North

The reconceptualization suggested above must be supported by policy catalysts that open the way for accelerated recovery with transformation. These lead policy actions within Africa and at the international level are essentially complementary, and need to be pursued within the framework of the emerging consensus on adjustment.

Policy changes in Africa

(1) *Political will and self-confidence* – The first major policy shift in Africa at both national and regional levels involves the generation of the political will and self-confidence required to pursue the "willed future" of the normative trends scenario. This is the most fundamental challenge facing Africa and its leaders. They must find the courage, determination and confidence to defend their resolutions and implement their own blueprints. The absence of these has been the singular and most daunting tragedy of Africa. Hence it is a challenge to the people at large – their trade unions, NGOs, business, peasant, women, youth, students and professional associations must demand this political steadfastness from African leaders. They cannot, and should not, be allowed to say or sign one thing and do the other. There must be sustained pressure from below to make African leaders responsive to the popular will and sincere to their public commitments. It is the absence of these political obligations that led to the failure to implement the Lagos Plan of Action (LPA), the delay in embarking on the normative trends scenario since 1983 and the continuation of orthodox SAPs for so long despite their disastrous failure.

(2) *Implementation of AAF–SAP* – The necessary steps must be urgently initiated for the effective implementation of the laudable strategies and policy measures for achieving Africa's long-term development objectives as detailed in the African Alternative Framework (AAF–SAP). This requires mounting the detailed country studies for the design of national policy packages as a follow-up to the preparation of AAF-SAP and its Selected Policy Instruments. Then the policy packages should be implemented in each country through the mobilization of domestic resources and their efficient utilization. African countries should collectively call upon the Bretton Woods institutions and the rest of the international community to honour their repeated pledges to support the initiative and leadership of African countries in the recovery process. Africa must occupy the driver's seat in the adjustment-with-transformation exercise and each African country should design its own programme which the IMF and World Bank should assist and support – rather than

hijacking the initiative from Africa. The lesson of the non-implementation of the LPA should be warning enough of the imperative to implement AAF–SAP through national and collective regional initiatives.

(3) *Democratization, accountability and peace* – These should be accepted as basic pre-conditions for genuine development in Africa. The effective mobilization and utilization of domestic resources demand them. In particular, the corruption in many African countries with massive export of capital must be arrested through concerted action by the people and their organizations, the enforcement of financial and political accountability and the plugging of leakages. The resolution of widespread internal conflicts and strife with their horrendous refugee problem is critical, and the OAU and sub-regional groupings (ECOWAS, PTA, etc.) have a major mediation role to play here.

(4) *Commodity problem, debt, reparations and delinking* – These are united by the common thread of resource constraint for Africa's development. Determined collective action is required to ensure progress on them, particularly because they involve political initiatives and regional cooperation, e.g., to pursue selective disengagement, closure or delinking. The major issues involved in each of them have been analysed and it remains here only to underscore the concerted political programme required for their successful pursuit. On-going initiatives in the Frazer Report on *Africa's Commodity Problems* and other proposals for drastic external debt relief should be urgently implemented without further foot-dragging.

International policy shifts

The international policy shifts required from the Bretton Woods institutions, other development and financial agencies, bilateral donors and the rest of the international community are:

(1) *External Debt Action* – The international community should demonstrate its commitment to be Africa's effective development partners in the 1990s by *implementing*, not just announcing, drastic external debt relief actions. Africa and the rest of the Third World have waited for 10 long years for this and the promised debt relief should be operational by now. If the tortuous negotiations and foot-dragging on these debts are suggestions of Western refusal to free Africa from debt peonage, then African countries should take collective action to veto the decision. Without the resolution of the

external debt crisis, no international commitment, including increased resource flows to Africa, will amount to much, as most of the additional inflows will simply be swallowed up in rising foreign debt service payments with little left for development.

(2) *Solutions to Commodity Problems* – The establishment of the Frazer Committee on these problems by the UN is appreciated, but this has been betrayed by the utterly useless report of the Committee. So the UN and the rest of the international community should take urgent steps to implement *Africa's Common Position on the Frazer Report.* The imminent approach of Europe 1992 and increasing economic regionalism make the early resolution of this problem critical for Africa. Fundamental policy shifts involving concessionary access to foreign markets for Africa's traditional and manufactured exports, revival of suspended or scrapped International Commodity Agreements, augmentation of compensatory foreign trade financing under an enlarged International Commodity Fund, without conditionality, and modifications of the Lomé IV as it affects Africa's agricultural and other exports, are among the required policy actions.

(3) *Uruguay Round of GATT* – These talks will impose net financial losses of around $3 billion annually, eliminate the "development principle" that accords special concessions for development, e.g., protection of infant industries, increase foreign exploitation of African countries by multinational corporations (MNCs) through the deregulation of foreign trade in investment, technology and services as proposed in "trade-related investment measures" (TRIMs) and "trade-related intellectual property rights" (TRIPs on technology), and cause enormous environmental hazards through deforestation for timber, loss of control over food hazards, e.g. hormones in meat, etc. (Ragavan, 1990). Hence the proposed liberalization of world trade proposed in the Uruguay Round of GATT should be shelved. African countries should reject it because it will worsen the region's international trade situation and aggravate its horrendous environmental degradation.

(4) *International Support for Africa and Financial Flows* – the international community should also actively support Africa's pursuit of the normative trends scenario in two concrete ways. One is by visibly allowing African countries to conceptualize and design their own recovery-with-transformation programmes rather than imposing IMF-World Bank orthodox SAPs on them. As these foisted programmes have failed everywhere, Africa's development partners

should support, rather than displace and supplant, Africa's blueprints for its own recovery and development. The Bretton Woods institutions can assist the formulation of such national programmes along with the ECA, but they should not veto and reject national initiatives. The refusal to support such national initiatives open the IMF and World Bank to accusations of undermining the sovereignty of African countries, supervising their recolonization and serving imperial interests in these countries – all of which are contrary to their mandate. They should assist African countries with technical and financial support for the design and implementation of national programmes for recovery-with-transformation on the basis of AAF-SAP. *Additional* net resource inflows on concessionary terms are another way of supporting Africa's development. The emphasis is on additionality – over and above foreign debt service payments. This requires the immediate termination of *net* resource outflows from Africa to the North, the reversal of the annual *net* transfer of over $1 billion from African countries to the IMF and World Bank since 1987, and the creation of a *Special Transformation Fund* for Africa similar to the $14 billion OECD Fund for Eastern Europe. Conditionalities that inhibit drawing from existing funds like ESAF, International Commodity Fund, aid under Lomé IV etc., should also be removed to facilitate access and the additionality of resource inflows.

Chapter 8
Africa's second coming in a world in transition

There are important parallels between the 1960s and the 1990s for Africa. In both decades, the region was terminating colonial domination with the old Colonialism of the 1960s giving way to political independence, while the "new Colonialism" that has been imposed since the 1980s is being challenged by a new political and economic offensive defined round the democratic upsurge and the African Alternative Framework (AAF-SAP). In both decades, a "wind of change" has been blowing across the continent and sweeping away entrenched and repressive regimes under the pressure of a broad-based democratic zeal. There is a strong determination in both cases to change the course of the region's recent humiliating history and its exploitative foreign subordination. The 1960s inherited the disarticulated and debilitating political and economic structures of the Colonial interventionist state and the 1990s stand on its ruinous remains. The wreckage of the repressive one-party state and the pervasive denial of democracy stand atop the disastrous failure of IMF-World Bank orthodox stabilization and structural adjustment programmes. The profound confusion of values and institutions from colonialism almost parallel the current decay of values and institutions. The massive demonstrations and incessant chanting of FREEDOM! FREEDOM!! that rent the air in the 1960s can almost be heard now in every corner of Africa.

Yet there are significant differences between the two decades. The colonial world and its absolute dictators have given way to a world in transition in the 1990s. There is a significant benefit of hindsight and accumulated lessons of experience, especially from the catastrophe of the 1980s, to guide the future into the 21st century. There are now numerous blueprints on the major issues of the day to inspire and guide change. The profound sense of uncertainty of the 1960s is much less profound today. The social forces in the two contexts have also changed qualitatively from petty-bourgeios nationalists to pro-democracy and revolutionary masses – though they are still very much under the leadership of the same old social strata. This time around, there are also two countervailing factors on the world stage. One is the increasing hostility of the international economic environment underscored by the deepening crisis of world capitalism, the foreign debt crisis, the collapse of Africa's commodity trade and the coming of Europe 1992. The other factor is that Africa's second coming is part of a World Democratic Revolution-in-process that should offer it greater legitimacy and international support, especially from Western democracies, unlike the era of global schism during the Cold War of the 1960s. But this harbours a major disadvantage in that the Socialist Bloc that was the ready ally of Africa and the rest of the Third World from the 1960s is undergoing basic reforms and no longer in a strong position to assist. Some even assert that the Socialist Bloc has simply deserted Africa and left it stranded to whatever fate world capitalism may have in store for it. Putting the two factors together, Africa wins one plus in the world democratic upsurge, but registers two minuses in the growing hostility of the international economic environment and the weakened support of the Socialist Bloc.

Transformation not stagnation

With the benefit of hindsight and the bitter lessons of the lost decade of the 1980s, Africa has to make a definitive and fundamental choice about its future destiny. This is to choose accelerated recovery-with-transformation rather than stagnation and decline. One generation has already been lost to the crisis and that must end the loss and retrogression. Africa must resolve henceforth to relaunch its development that was interrupted in the 1980s. It has already resolved symbolically to do so by formulating and collectively adopting the *African Alternative Framework* (AAF-SAP) to orthodox SAPs; by preparing to ratify the Draft Treaty establishing the African Economic Community in June 1991; by adopting the *African Charter for Popular Participation in Development* (ACPPD); and by adopting a *Common Position on the Frazer Report on Africa's Commodity Problems* and a *Common Position on External Debt*. These are sufficient blueprints for launching the second coming of Africa.

But adopting and ratifying programmes and documents will not be enough this time around. Cynics will insist that the Lagos Plan of Action and several protocols have been adopted collectively without being implemented in the past, and that these may be no different. They must be proven wrong by a decisive shift if Africa is to survive – let alone develop. *Can Africa Survive*? by Basil Davidson, a well-meaning liberal friend of Africa, has raised the warning. In the 1990s, the very physical survival of 600 million Africans is at stake and therefore these blueprints must be effectively implemented. The World Democratic Movement is blowing a new wind of change that threatens to escalate into a political hurricane if things do not change fast enough. New social forces that have been created since the 1960s are both demanding change and poised for the transformation of African countries. So the old resistance and crusted decay must be swept aside. The damning implications of the Single Europe Market by 1992 and other emerging regional economic blocs will drum the inevitable beat of dialectics even into absolutely deaf ears, leaving no illusions about the imperative necessity for change. The chime of "aid fatigue" in the West will impose the necessity for increasing self-reliance, both national and collective. Yes, Africa has no choice but to swim – it cannot afford to sink – because the stakes are too high and the resistance to sinking is too great and mounting within the African masses.

The "willed future" of the normative trends scenario of sustained development must be Africa's unfaltering goal in the 1990s and beyond. The challenges for its achievement centre fundamentally on the promotion of *alternative cultural values* in the widest sense – a new political culture embracing a new kind of leadership that is honest, patriotic and responsive; the full democratization of society with the observance of democratic rights and political tolerance; and a vigilant and politically informed population. There has to be a new vision, a sense of purpose and a determination to succeed. Africa is not inherently deficient in these cultural values – but they have to be mobilized and applied for the urgent task of recovery-with-transformation.

The growing marginalization of Africa on all fronts must finally drive home the imperative necessity for change. Africa has adjusted massively at all levels and at immense physical and human costs. Yet, from the position of net exporter of food in an agricultural region, it has become a highly indebted net importer of food; its share of world exports has fallen from 4.7 per cent in 1980 to 2.1 per cent in 1988–89; and its share of world industrial production has also declined to below 1 per cent by 1989 despite the first Industrial Development Decade for Africa (IDDA I). The juxtaposition of increasing adjustment and growing marginalization thus underscores a policy gap, with which the regional blueprints are attempting to deal. Hence the real challenge of achieving Africa's willed future lies in the implementation of alternative policies for recovery and development.

This raises the relative power of internal strength and the international environment. For practical purposes, the external setting of Africa's development must be taken as exogenous and not amenable to control from the region. Hence the primacy of focusing on the internal dynamics of the structural transformation of African countries. Charity for Africa must, therefore, begin from home. Contrary to the pessimism of cynics, a lot can be done within Africa and regional strength is far greater than is often supposed. The enormous human resources, mineral wealth and agricultural potentials can be harnessed more imaginatively and utilized more efficiently to initiate an irreversible process of regional transformation that must start now.

Optimism and internal strength

The second coming of Africa must be heralded with one deafening slogan: "Optimism and Internal Strength". The salvation of Africa lies primarily in Africa and with Africans themselves. Optimism must become a resounding virtue and widely disseminated psychological trait – even in the face of challenges. Despair and pessimism are very tempting in Africa under SAP, but they are the very negation of determination and the falsification of hope. Pessimism is self-defeating fatalism. Robust optimism about Africa's future is a major requirement for the *self-confidence* that Africans need so badly to deal with the challenges of this historical juncture. Regardless of what Africa's detractors may say or do, Africans themselves must never lose faith in their own capacity and ability to change the course of events – to achieve the willed future for themselves.

We appreciate the difference between optimism and illusion or self-deception. Nobody denies that the odds against Africa, both internal and external, are immense, or that the situation has been deteriorating for a long time. But one of the lessons of economic history is that other regions, peoples and countries have survived this type of malaise. To cite a few examples, the Soviet Union, China and even the USA were the playgrounds of international adventurers for years before their peoples pulled themselves together and struck a breakthrough. Japan, our modern economic miracle, was a write-off before the Tokugawa era and the Meijti Restoration. Even Turkey before Ataturk was given up as lost. Europe under Hitler could easily have been given up during the Second World War. But these are all flourishing civilizations today, and so Africa can be. The Chinese insist that even a thousand mile journey must start with the first step – Africa's current blueprints can be regarded as the first step that must be followed up by a second.

The utility of rebounding optimism about Africa's future must lie primarily in a grim determination to muster effective *internal strength* from the cluster of existing resources – people, materials, ideas and programmes. If the optimism is not associated with conscious and vigorous effort to build this strength within Africa, it will be no more than wishful thinking. In the context of the argumentation in this book, the mobilization of this domestic might involves four critical factors.

One is the acceptance of the responsibility to *lead* the salvation, recovery and transformation of the region by Africans themselves. Europeans developed Europe; Soviets developed the USSR; Americans transformed the USA; and the Japanese transformed Japan. So only the Africans themselves can develop Africa – nobody else can or will do it. Africans themselves must occupy the driver's seat in the recovery and transformation of the region. This is where the on-going orthodox SAPs are patently wrong. Throughout economic history, it has never been recorded that foreigners designed and directed the successful development of any part of the world as the IMF and World Bank claim that they can do in Africa with their SAPs. And this must be quite clear – these foreigners can only manipulate Africa and at best achieve some temporary relief with marginal growth here and there. They cannot, and they will not, permanently transform Africa – if only because that will threaten their global strategy and basic interests. The realization of this fact is part of the beginning of wisdom for Africa – no people, country or region ever develops another. Sustainable development is always primarily an internal effort as a matter of self-development. Foreigners can only assist it – they cannot lead it or substitute for the indigens because of the inevitable clash of domestic and foreign interests. So Africa must lead and effectively control its development process – it must insist on conceptualizing the process, designing and implementing it – with assistance and support from outside.

The second requirement is a *vision* of the willed future or desired state. This must be the collective and, therefore, democratic articulation of the aspirations and destiny sought by a people or region. What kind of Africa and Africans do we want to see ten, thirty, fifty or a hundred years from now? What should Africa's role be in world affairs by then and how should it relate to the rest of the world? In what stages and with what strategies is the desired future state to be achieved? What are the major obstacles, internal and external, that will have to be dealt with, etc? All these will together constitute the elements of a collective blueprint that will elaborate Africa's vision. Happily, Africa articulated such a vision as far back as 1980. But any such vision must guide and inspire policy action – it must be implemented – and this is Africa's greatest failing so far.

There is then need for *self-pride and self-respect* for standing by the articulated vision. Without this, the rest of the world cannot take Africa seriously, or respect the continent and its peoples. This requires Africa to defend and implement its vision, programmes and resolutions, even in the face of obstacles and criticism. Integrity and accountability are critical here. They demand a sense of patriotism, a refusal to swindle one's country for personal enrichment, or to betray one's nation and the loyalty of the people. Self-respecting people will not routinely inflate contracts for corrupt enrichment, wantonly abuse their office or refuse to impose sanctions on those who violate their rules. Basic mutual trust among African countries will develop with this integrity and patriotic commitment to the cause of the continent and its peoples. This self-respect is also inconsistent with what has been called the *three-lenses syndrome*, according to which foreigners define how Africans see themselves; how Africans see the rest of the world; and how the rest of the world should see Africa. This must be jettisoned if Africans must lead their development process with their own vision.

The fourth element is that the greatest source of internal strength lies simply in *unity*, cooperation and integration. A house divided against itself cannot stand, and this is why pervasive conflicts and strife have been so debilitating in Africa, and must be resolved for the challenges of the 1990s. With growing economic regionalism the world over, "*Africa must unite*" as the late President Nkrumah of Ghana used to urge. As the most vulnerable and most fragmented region in the world, effective integration is the only real hope for Africa. The illusion of independent national development must be jettisoned as a bad joke in a region where nine countries have populations less than one million and 24 others have less than 10 million.

Critical challenges for Africa's second coming

One-word captions for social phenomena are usually over-simplified and suspect. Yet, many are tempted to sum up Africa's central problem as *leadership*. The direct correlation between bad politics and growing poverty in Africa also means that poor and even disastrous political leadership has been a major factor in the intensification of poverty, under-development and crisis in the region. When people think of massive capital flight, they see a leadership problem, especially when some national leaders are directly accused of swindling billions of dollars from their countries and stashing them abroad in secret bank accounts (Naylor, 1988). When they discuss widespread lack of accountability and democracy that throttles development, political leadership is also prominent. Leadership also plays a central role in the accumulation of unpayable foreign debts, distorted national priorities, non-implementation of the LPA and other approved programmes, unproductive investment, excessive defence spending and pervasive internal conflicts, which have all contributed significantly to the current crisis. Africans are loudly saying that they want a different kind of leadership for the 1990s. Needless to say, that leadership is gradually emerging from the ruins of the dictators that dot Africa, and from the on-going people's democratic offensive for effective popular participation in decision-making, resource allocation and the equitable distribution of the benefits of development. People's empowerment is slowly but gradually catching on, though there is still far to go.

Similarly, sustained *political will and self-confidence* of both leaders and the people are critical for the successful second coming of Africa. Though the political will is narrowly that of the top political leadership, pressure from the people is very important in generating it. Clearly if the people remain apathetic and indifferent, the leaders will do as they please. So the people must organize themselves at all levels as a social force to gear their leaders to support this or that, and to stop this policy or another. This pressure from trade unions, peasant, women, youth, student and professional associations has been decisive in galvanizing the necessary political will for the realization of the European Community. Africa must also mobilize the self-confidence to stick by its resolutions, policies and programmes. The depth of the current crisis has been due partly to this singular failure to implement national, sub-regional and regional decisions, protocols and programmes with respect to the development aspirations of the continent. Here again, the people have an important role to ensure their leaders implement these policies. When this is not done, the people and the media must not only give reminders but press for action through massive popular demand and activism.

All these are central to the urgent and effective implementation of the *African Alternative Framework* (AAF-SAP) to orthodox SAPs and of African integration at sub-regional and regional levels. If foreigners cannot develop Africa, the failed on-going SAPs have been shown empirically to be incapable of achieving recovery-with-transformation for Africa. After ten years, these orthodox SAPs are still said to be evolving – implying clearly that African countries are being used as mere guinea pigs for costly international policy experiments. If, after ten years, short-term stabilization has not been achieved with these programmes, African countries must urgently replace them with the more relevant African Alternative Framework. As Africans must assume the leadership of their own development and articulate their vision of that transformation, orthodox SAPs must be replaced with national policy packages based on AAF-SAP. The political will and self-confidence required for the second coming of Africa must be demonstrated by initiating the steps for the country study as a follow-up to *AAF-SAP Selected Policy Instruments*, and for designing and implementing alternative policy packages for recovery-with-transformation.

Similarly, African countries must take urgent steps to ratify the Draft Treaty of the African Economic Community and shorten its implementation timetable to some 10 years. The disappointment with Lomé IV, the imminent threat of Europe 1992 and the challenges of other regional economic blocs must be fully exploited to accelerate the implementation of the African Community. Its funding should be boosted beyond member-state contributions and the broad social forces of trade unions, Chambers of Commerce, NGOs, women and other social associations should be fully mobilized for its implementation. This also requires strengthening the sub-regional groupings, rationalizing mini-groupings and the large number of around 200 inter-governmental organizations (IGOs) in the region. The political pre-conditions for closer integration, especially the resolution of internal conflicts and strife as well as broad popular participation should also be vigorously pursued.

Support of the international community

Though Africa and Africans must take the leading role in the region's recovery and transformation from the 1990s, the support of the international community is important as discussed in the previous chapter. The two urgent areas for this international action are drastic external debt relief and the expansion of Africa's commodity trade as outlined in the OAU's Common Position on the Frazer Report on Africa's Commodity Problems. Without a resolution of these external constraints, sustainable development in the 1990s will be very difficult in African countries. Again, what is required is not new decision-making as such, but the implementation of existing decisions on these central questions.

A special external role that will be required in the 1990s is a departure from the trend of systematic subordination and displacement of African initiative in the 1980s. Africa needs external support and assistance – not the displacement of its initiatives, greater subordination and recolonization. In particular, the international community should bring greater pressure to bear on the IMF and World Bank to implement existing consensus on adjustment by providing financial and technical assistance for the urgent implementation of AAF-SAP. As required by its *Long-term Perspective Study* (LTPS), the World Bank should redirect scarce resources from duplicating blueprints for Africa into supporting the implementation of Africa's own blueprints. This is the way to be faithful to the often-repeated claims of the Bretton Woods institutions that they are only supportive of the sovereign initiatives of African countries.

Western countries can also facilitate the success of Africa's second coming in the 1990s by sincerely supporting the democratization process on the continent. They should do this by terminating their critical support for dictatorial and repressive regimes in many African countries. They must refrain from the hypocrisy and double-standard of proclaiming democracy at home and championing dictatorship and fascism in African countries. Africa has adopted a Charter for Popular Participation and counts on the West in particular for support in implementing it successfully – as the democratic reforms in Eastern Europe were supported.

Environmental protection is a rapidly growing agenda in Africa, especially in the 1990s and beyond. The recent global report on our *Common Future* summarizes the major global consensus which the 1992 UN Conference on Environment and Development (UNCED-1992) is to pursue. Africa will need major international support in these contexts for coping with its massive environmental degradation because it harbours the largest desert land area in the world with severe desertification. Drought in the Sahel is also a peculiar environmental problem in Africa. The grinding poverty in the region directly exacerbates these environmental problems which require massive international assistance to terminate. The scope of Africa's environmental degradation has been firmly established to be beyond the scope of the dwindling resources of any one country or of Africa as a whole. This is one clear area of global cooperation and solidarity in the 1990s.

Reform of the IMF and World Bank

Africa and the rest of the developing world are greatly dissatisfied with the operations of the IMF and World Bank and their high profile as new colonizers. There have been numerous conflicts and disagreements between the Bretton Woods institutions and several developing countries, especially in the 1980s, over conditionality and cross-conditionality, orthodox SAPs and evaluation reports (Payer, 1982). In addition, within the staff of the Fund and Bank, there are strong divisions on these issues – and some staff have resigned angrily in protest against the Fund and Bank and published their protests. Two examples of such resignation protests are by Davidson L. Budhoo, a former senior IMF Consultant from Trinidad, who produced a twenty-page resignation letter from the IMF in 1989 and expanded it into a book titled: *Dear Mr. Camdessus*[1] *– Enough is Enough* (Budhoo, 1990); and Michael Irwin who resigned as Acting Vice-President from the Personnel Department of the World Bank in 1989–90. He stated that the Bank "could do twice as much with its present staff or only needed half the staff for the present workload"; and that the Bank pays its staff 40 to 60 per cent more than the UN (Irwin, 1990). Budhoo accused the IMF of manipulating data from Trinidad and Tobago, the government appointed an international body to investigate the allegation and it was confirmed (*Ibid*, pp. 4 and 43–7).

Budhoo has made some detailed proposals for the reform of the Fund and Bank which we share and, therefore, present in the reform proposals below (*Ibid*, pp. 48–52 and 82–94). They centre on four basic issues, namely: the democratization of the Fund and Bank; rehabilitation of their very unsatisfactory resource transfer procedures and record; frequent conflicts in relations with developing member countries; and the excessive power and remuneration of their bloated bureaucracy – in institutions that tirelessly berate developing countries for over-staffing and impose massive retrenchment on them (Payer, *op. cit*, Ch. 13). The main reform proposals are:

Democratisation of Fund and Bank

Voting rights and the formal control of the Fund and Bank are monopolized by the countries of Western Europe and North America – even excluding Japan. Thus the President of the World Bank is by convention always from the USA and the Managing Director of the IMF is always from Western Europe. Together these Atlantic countries control around 80 per cent of the voting rights of these institutions by dominating their Board of Governors and Board of Executive Directors. Hence the need to upgrade the status of developing countries as owners of the Fund and Bank to reflect not

1. Mr Camdessus is the Managing Director of the IMF.

only their quota contributions but also their share of transactions as users of the resources of these institutions, major sources of their profits and originators of most of their business. Thus even though the advanced countries took about 70 per cent of the loans of these institutions between 1944 and 1978, the developing countries have been taking that share of the loans since then, with Africa alone making net transfers of over $1 billion to these institutions annually from 1987. This democratization along with the overhauling of the entire Bretton Woods international economic and financial system that has been in crisis since the 1960s demands another major international conference similar to that of Bretton Woods in 1944;

Resource transfer procedures

The Bank has made wide incursions beyond the intentions of its 1944 Articles of Agreement in resource transfer to developing countries through its strong thrust into socio-economic lending (education, health, rural development, population, etc.); expansion of country over project technical assistance on its own account and as an Executing Agency for other institutions; and increasing involvement in aid coordination for the international community. These require the following checks and balances (also applicable to the Fund):

Fund Council
Independent and with broad decision-making powers to replace the toothless Interim Committee, Development Committee and Group of Twenty-Four in the Fund's Articles of Agreement of 1944. This Fund Council should not depend on Fund staff but have its own technical expertise as a counterweight to the staff of the Fund;

Independent Advisory Bodies for the Bank
These are stipulated in the Bank's Articles of Agreement to play intermediating roles in decision-making. These bodies are to include:

- an advisory council – selected by the Board of Governors to include representatives of banking, commercial, industrial, labour and agricultural interests . . . with as wide a national representation as possible;
- each loan committee of the Bank to also "include an expert selected by the Governor representing the member in whose territory the project is located". But none of these mechanisms are operational at present.

Relations with Member States

These require new organs to deal with frequent and increasing conflicts. They should include:

Advisory and Review Commission

This should be a final court of appeal in (a) disputes between Fund–Bank and member countries over policy changes required to achieve particular economic and social objectives in projects where Fund–Bank resources are involved; (b) charges of bias, inconsistency etc. by member countries against the Fund–Bank, e.g. in its evaluation reports; (c) complaints by Fund–Bank against member countries for non-compliance with agreed conditionality in programmes;

Regional Coordinating Committees

These should be created as parallels to the many Regional Offices or Departments of the Fund–Bank. Each Committee should undertake a "country economic review" after receiving a Fund–Bank Country Economic Report or similar document. Only nationals of the region served by each Committee should be eligible for election – by Fund–Bank Governors for the region and Governors from other regions;

Programme Watch Committee

Developing countries themselves should urgently establish this Committee in each country to oversee their interests in negotiations with Fund–Bank. This Watch Committee should be composed of representatives of governments, NGOs, trade unions, peasants, women and professional associations to monitor negotiations with the Fund–Bank, evaluate policies and programmes as well as monitor loans (amounts, disbursement, uses, etc.). The Committee should terminate the revolting and undemocratic secrecy of Fund–Bank dealings with member countries;

Environmental Impact Assessment Committees

These should function alongside the Regional Coordinating Committees and have at least one member on the Watch Committee. They should be composed of nationals of each region where there are Fund–Bank Regional Offices or Departments and they should be elected from the ranks of environmentalists, economists, NGOs and trade unions.

They should monitor the ecological impact of Fund–Bank programmes like dams/irrigation, mineral, industrial and other projects to ensure environmental accounting.

Restriction of Fund–Bank Staff Powers and Renumerations

Michael Irwin (*Ibid*) reported that Fund–Bank staff salaries of over

$120,000 per annum, excluding fringe benefits, are about 40–60 per cent higher than those of the staff of other UN agencies and that the Bank's staff could be reduced by about 50 per cent without decreasing performance. Their absolute powers in dealings with member countries should also be drastically curtailed – they should have no direct access to Heads of State, and only their senior staff should have direct access to State Ministers. The above internal and external checks and balances should clip the large and colonial wings of Fund–Bank staff.

In these ways, the Fund and Bank would become less authoritarian, more responsive to the needs of *humane development* and of the majority of poor and rural peoples, and their activities should become more open, less suspicious and less manipulative. These are urgently required to facilitate the re-orientation and response of the Bretton Woods institutions to the changed requirements of human-centred development from those of the Second World War to the new reality at the threshold of the 21st century. Africa, in particular, should press for these Fund–Bank reforms because it suffers most from the abuses of the absolute power of these institutions and their authoritarian practices.

References

Adedeji, Adebayo (1989) *Towards a Dynamic African Economy* (London: Frank Cass).

Adedeji, Adebayo (1990) "Preliminary Assessment of the Performance of the African Economy, 1989"; Press release (Addis Ababa).

Adedeji, Adebayo (1990) *The African Alternative* (Addis Ababa).

Adedeji, Adebayo and Timothy Shaw, eds. (1985) *Economic Crisis in Africa – African Perspectives in Development Problems and Potentials* (Colorado).

African Development Bank, *African Development Report*, 1990 (Abidjan).

Alavi, H. (1972) 'The Post-colonial State', New Left Review 74.

Amin, Samir (1972) *Accumulation on a World Scale – Critique of the Theory of Underdevelopment*, vols. I & II (New York: Monthly Review Press).

—— (1990) *Delinking – Towards a Polycentric World* (Zed Books, London).

Babu, M. (1981) *African Socialism or Socialist Africa* (Zed Books, London).

Budhoo, D.L. (1990) *Dear Mr. Camdessus – Enough is Enough* (New York: New Horizon Press).

Cimade, I. and K. Min (1986) *The African Refugee Crisis* (London: Zed).

Concord Press (1990) International Conference on Reparations Payment to Africa and the Diaspora, December 13–14, 1990.

Concord Press (1990) *Proceedings of International Conference on Reparations Payment to Africa and Diaspora (Lagos)*, December 14–15.

Daily Times of Nigeria, April 24, 1990.

ECA (1983) *Long-term Perspectives of the African Economy* (Addis Ababa).

ECA (1983) *Long-term Perspective on African Development* (Addis Ababa).

ECA (1986) *African Priority Programme for Economic Recovery (APPER)* (Addis Ababa).

ECA (1987) *The Kilimanjaro Programme of Action on* Africa's Population Problems and the *Khartoum Declaration* on the Human Dimension of Adjustment, 1988 (Addis Ababa).

ECA (1988) *Revised Long-term Perspective on African Development from 1983 to Year 2008* (Addis Ababa).

ECA (1989) *Abuja Declaration on Women* (Addis Ababa).

ECA (1989) *The African Alternative Framework to Structural Adjustment Programmes for Socio-Economic Recovery and Transformation* (AAF-SAP), Addis Ababa.

ECA (1989) *The Kampala Agenda for Action on Environment* (Addis Ababa).

ECA (1989) *Statistics and Policies* (Addis Ababa).

ECA (1990) *Economic Report on Africa*, (Addis Ababa).

ECA (1991) *AAF-SAP* – Selected Policy Instruments (Addis Ababa).

EEC/ACP (1990) *Lomé IV Convention* (Brussels).

ECA/OAU/World Bank (1989) *Joint Statement* on Africa's Recovery (Washington), May 10.

Eringer, Robert (1981) *The Global Manipulators – Covert Power Groups of the West* (Bristol: Pentacle Books).

FAO (1988) *Estimates of Africa's Food Requirements* (Rome).

Fitt, Y. *et al* (1980) *The World Economic Crisis – US Imperialism at Bay* (Zed Press, London).

Frank, A. G. (1974) *Latin America – Underdevelopment or Revolution* (New York: Monthly Review Press).

George, Susan (1988) *A Fate Worse than Debt* (London).

Government of Netherlands (1990), *Maastricht Conference* (Maastricht and The Hague).

Gutkind, P.C.W. and Wallerstein, I. (eds) (1976) *The Political Economy of Contemporary Africa* (Sage Publications).

IFAA (1988) The IMF, World Bank and the Africa Debt (conference report).

ILO, *International Labour Review*, Various Issues since the 1980s (Geneva).

Irwin, Michael (1990) Resignation Letter from the World Bank in *Inside the World Bank* (IFAA Publications, London).

Jolly, R et al. (1987) *Adjustment with a Human Face* (Oxford University Press).

Knudsen, O. *et al* (1989) *Agricultural Policies and Developing Countries* (Washington).

Lowi, T.J. (1969) *The End of Liberalism* (New York: Norton & Co.).

Mahjoub, A. ed. (1990) *Adjustment or De-Linking – The African Experience* (Tokyo: United Nations University Press and London: Zed Books) p. 167.

Mandel, E. (1980) *The Second Slump* (London: Verso).

Marx, Karl (1970) *On Colonialism* (Moscow: Progress Publishers).

Naylor, R.T. (1988) *Hot Money and the Politics of Debt* (London).

Newswatch Magazine, June–September 1989 (Lagos).

Nyongo, P.A. ed. (1987) *Popular Struggles for Democracy in Africa* (London: United Nations University and Zed Books).

Nyongo, P.A. (1990) *African Integration – Unfinished Agenda* (Nairobi; African Academy of Sciences).

OAU (1981) *African Charter on Human and People's Rights* (Addis Ababa).

OAU, *African Common Position on External Debt and Common Position on the Frazer Report on Africa's Commodity Problems and Treaty of the African Economic Community,* AEC (Addis Ababa).

OAU (1981) *The Lagos Plan of Action for African Economic Development from 1980 to year 2000*, (LPA), Addis Ababa.

Onimode, Bade (1982) *Imperialism and Underdevelopment in Nigeria* (London: Zed).

Onimode, Bade (1988) *Report of IFAA's 1987 Conference* on Impact of IMF/World Bank Programmes on the People of Africa (London).

Onimode, Bade (1988) *A Political Economy of the African Crisis* (London: IFAA and Zed).

Onimode, Bade, ed. (1989) *The I.M.F., World Bank and the African Debt: Vol. 1, Economic Impact; Vol. II, Social and Political Impact* (London: IFAA and Zed).

Payer, Cheryl (1974) *The Debt Trap – The IMF and The Developing Countries* (New York: Monthly Review Press).

—— (1982) 'The World Bank – A critical analysis', *New York Monthly Review*.

Poulantzas, N. (1975) *Classes in Contemporary Capitalism* (London).

Ragavan, C. (1989) *Recolonisation – the Uruguary Round of GATT and the Third World* (Penang: Third World Network).

Rodney, Walter (1970) *A History of the Upper Guinea Coast 1545 to 1800* (New York: Monthly Review Press).

Rodney, Walter (1972) *How Europe Underdeveloped Africa* (Dar es Salaam: Tanzania Publishing House).

Smith, Adam (1970) *The Wealth of Nations* (Penguin Books, London).

The South Commission (1990) *The Challenge to the South – The Report of the South Commission* (Oxford University Press).

Taylor, Lance, ed. (1987) *Varieties of Stabilisation Experience* (Oxford University Press).

United Nations (1987) *Our Common Future*, Report on UN World Commission on Environment and Development (New York).

United Nations (1990) *Frazer Report on Africa's Commodity Problems – The Solutions* (New York).

UNDP (1990) *Human Development Report, 1990* (New York).

Vaitsos, C. (1970) "Transfer of Resources and Preservation of Monopoly Rents", Economic Development Report number 168, Centre for International Affairs, Harvard University.

Williams, Eric (1972) *Capitalism and Slavery* (Johns Hopkins University Press).

World Bank (1981) *Towards Accelerated Development in Sub-Saharan Africa* (Berg Report), Washington.

World Bank (1987) *Sub-Saharan Africa: From Crisis to Sustainable Growth – A Long-term Perspective Study (LTPS)*, Washington.

World Bank, *World Development Report 1987* (Washington DC).

World Bank (1989) *Sub-Saharan Africa: From Crisis to Sustainable Growth – A Long-term Perspective Study (LTPS),* Washington.

World Bank (1988) Varieties of Stabilization Experience, World Institute for Development Economics Research (WIDER), (Oxford).

World Bank, *World Debt Tables, 1988–89* (Washington).

World Bank, *World Development Report 1989* (Washington).

World Bank *World Development Report, 1990 – Poverty* (Washington).

World Bank (1990) *African Capacity Building Initiative,* ACBI (Washington).

The World Bank's Assessment of its SAPs are contained in its following publications: (1) (1988) *Adjustment Lending – An Evaluation of Ten Years of Experience*; (2) (1988) *Africa's Adjustment and Growth in the 1980s*; (3) World Development Report 1990 – *Poverty;* and (4) LTPS, *op.cit.*, Chapter 1.

The Evaluation of SAPs by the Nordic Countries was reported extensively in the following conference proceedings: K.J. Harnevik ed. (1987) *The IMF and The World Bank in Africa – Conditionality Impact and Alternatives* (Scandinavian Institute of African Studies).

Index